I0518491

TORN PAGES FROM A BROKEN HEART

Shattered by Grief,
Carried by Strength.

CJ INFANTINO

AN UNVOICED PRODUCTION
Released under Unvoiced LLC
New York

FIRST BOOK EDITION, SEPTEMBER 2025

Copyright © 2025 by CJ Infantino

This book is a work of memoir. It is a reflection of the author's personal experiences and recollections. Some names and identifying characteristics of individuals mentioned may have been changed to protect their privacy. The author and publisher have made every effort to ensure the accuracy of the information herein. However, the publisher and the author do not assume and hereby disclaim any liability to any party for any loss, damage, or disruption caused by errors or omissions, whether such errors or omissions result from negligence, accident, or any other cause. This book is not intended as a substitute for professional medical, psychological, or grief counseling advice. Readers should consult with a qualified professional for any specific concerns.

Published by:

Unvoiced LLC

Rochester, NY

www.unvoiced.com

Paperback ISBN: 979-8-9987468-1-9

Book design by Alicia Owen & CJ Infantino

Writing and images by CJ Infantino

To Grace, Charlie, and Cam

For their patience, endurance and forgiveness toward me.

CONTENTS

A BRIEF INTERMISSION

THE FIRST YEAR: CONTINUED

Ariana is gone.

Forever.

The kids lost their mother, and I lost my best friend.

We had no choice but to become motherless and wifeless.

We cannot change that.

So we move forward in it.

We lose ourselves.

We lose each other.

But somehow, we keep finding our way back.

I am a broken man with broken dreams, a broken body, and a broken heart.

For the first time in my life, I don't know how to pick up the pieces.

Each day is a labored survival, soaked in tears.

I am not a single parent.

I AM A WIDOWER

FOREWORD

Growing up in a family that revered strength, I learned early on that emotions were something to keep hidden. They weren't tools for success; they were obstacles. They had their place, but only behind closed doors, in private moments no one else could see. I carried that belief with me for years: that strength meant silence, and feeling too deeply made you weak.

I bring this up because I think many of us walk through life with that same weight. We're taught to curate ourselves: to smile when we're breaking, to be careful how much of our hearts we show. If we cry, we're "too sensitive." If we falter, we're "fragile." So we suppress the bad, exaggerate the good, armor up, and call that living.

Then I met CJ.

From the very beginning, I could feel there was something different about him. We met at the start of his journey with *Hopeless Mope*, a clothing brand that challenged everything I thought I knew about what it meant to be human. CJ created something that gave people permission to wear every part of themselves: the joy, sorrow, confusion, anger, all right there on their sleeves. The characters, the designs, the mission... it wasn't just fashion. It was a call to feel, and I was instantly sold.

But more than that, I was moved because this vision came from a place of unimaginable loss. Instead of turning inward, CJ chose to turn outward, using his grief not as a wall, but as a bridge to connect with others. That's just who he is. If you've ever wanted to know what selflessness looks like, look no further.

When I lost my dad, it was easy to fall back into old patterns: repress, ignore, move on. But CJ would hear my struggle and gently offer his reminder: *Let yourself feel.* I can't count how many times he's had to remind me, and I'm sure there will be many more, but those three words mean everything. It's a simple mantra, yet for someone who struggles deeply with emotions, it's a lifeline.

This is just one example of the way CJ impacts everyone he meets. There are people who talk about changing the world, and then there are people like CJ who *live* that change in every word, every breath, every action.

This book, *Torn Pages From A Broken Heart*, is a continuation of that selfless work. It's more than a book about grief; it's an invitation—a deeply personal, heartbreakingly honest doorway into the life of someone who lost everything and somehow found a way to keep going. Through these pages, CJ opens his heart, and in doing so, gives each of us courage to face our own hearts.

If you're grieving, you will feel seen.

If you're bracing for loss, you'll find the raw truth.

And if you stumbled across this book by chance, you'll find humanity.

CJ has impacted my life in more ways than I could properly recount here. But if this book gives you even a fraction of what he's given me, then you're about to be changed for the better. So as you read, remember that you are not only peering into the vulnerable heart of a fellow human; you are also allowing yourself to be vulnerable alongside him. Let this be your reminder that it's okay to feel. It's okay to be authentically you, no matter what that looks like.

The truth is, emotions don't make you less.

They make you human.

And CJ reminds us how beautiful, even in brokeness, that can be.

– Alicia Owen
Co-worker, Friend, Griever

PROLOGUE

GRIEF

Ariana was about a month into being a living science experiment, undergoing tests across her body for cancer. The latest test checked for cancer cells in her lymph nodes. A positive result would mean she was at stage three of her breast cancer diagnosis, indicating the cancer had likely broken through into other parts of her body.

The lymph node test involved shoving a long needle into her side to extract a tissue sample. It's as painful as it sounds. Ariana was not prone to voicing pain. Her threshold was unbelievably high, but when she returned from the test, she looked visibly affected.

If the next two tests came back negative, she would be curable at roughly a 90% rate. If not, she faced at best a low chance of cure, and at worst, incurable metastatic disease. A few days later, I was sitting in a team meeting at work when my phone rang. Looking at the screen, I noticed that it was Ariana. I excused myself from the meeting, walked outside the conference room and picked up.

"Hey," I said.

"Hey babe, so the test came back positive. They found cancer in my lymph nodes," Ariana spoke, unconcerned.

"Okay. How are you doing? What is the next step?"

"I'm okay. They will test my bones next week for the last test."

"Okay. Do you want me to come home?" I said.

"No. Finish work and I'll see you when you get home."

We said our goodbyes and hung up the phone. I stood for a moment to process what was happening. I wasn't sure if Ariana was grasping the reality of what these results meant or being strong for me. A positive result in her lymph nodes brought her dangerously close to incurability.

My stomach ached. My palms grew sweaty. I shook my head and slipped my phone into my pocket. I quietly opened the door to the conference room, walked in and sat down at the head of the table. The air escaped the room as my lungs constricted and struggled to function. The faces around the table that were staring at me quickly blurred behind the tears forming in my eyes.

"CJ, you okay, man?" one teammate asked, completely confused at what was happening. No one knew yet except my manager.

"No. I, uh." choking on my words. "Ariana has cancer and–um, well, we just got more tests back. I just want to let you guys know–that I, ah–I can't stay in California–I need to move back home. Ariana needs to be back home when she dies…" my voice trailed off.

No one spoke a word. They waited for someone to speak up and then, almost in unison, they said, "Oh my gosh, I'm so sorry, what can we do?"

Unable to answer, I felt the first heavy weight of grief begin to wrap and constrict around my heart. Weeks later, we were back in the oncologist's office after finding out her bones came back positive for cancer, and with that, her death sentence.

The office was quiet, and the last vestiges of the sun did

their best to bathe the waiting room with light. Few people were there. I sat to the right of Ariana, who was sandwiched between a fish tank and me. The air smelled sterile. I laid my head on Ariana's shoulder and held her hands in mine.

No words were spoken. Only incoherent sobs and cries. We did our best to control them. Failing more than we succeeded. I felt the first signs of my soul beginning to crack and break as I held her hand, knowing there was nothing I could do to protect my wife and my children's mother. I was helpless. This disease now controlled our lives.

All I could think about was how violently my future was taken from me. In just a few short years, my world would be taken from me. Her hands forever absent in mine. I would never see them old and wiry in our old age.

I thought about being a solo dad and raising my children through their teenage years. Alone. Helping them through their first loves. Their college applications. Watching them become adults. It was all on me. Everything. Providing. Praising. Instructing. Teaching. No one to collaborate with.

My thoughts were interrupted when I heard the nurse call out, "Ariana Infantino." We slowly walked back through the hallway, through the double doors, and then into the oncologist's office with enough space for a single patient and room enough for the oncologist's stool. We sat down on the two chairs squeezed to the side of the door. Our knees hitting the examination table and its roll of tissue paper that was somehow meant to keep it sterile. We sat, still crying. Still speechless.

The oncologist walked in, high-kneed her way to her stool, sat down with her back to us. She began running her fingers over the keyboard and in a few moments the screen was filled with Ariana's bone scans. She stared at them lifelessly. It felt as if she was counting the seconds, waiting until what felt like an appropriate amount of time to feign examining the results.

When the right number of moments had passed, she turned towards us and began explaining what was going on and what the results meant about Ariana's diagnosis.

"It is unfortunately stage four and the cancer has spread to your ribs and spine. We will treat you for quality of life rather than attempt to cure you."

I grabbed Ariana's hand and broke our silence, "How long does she have?" I asked.

"Well, I think with this diagnosis and where her tumors are, we can try to get close to ten years, but we really don't know. It's a very aggressive cancer. Some people have lived a few years and, rarely, some of my patients have gone 25 years." the oncologist said. Then without missing a beat, she leaned over, met our eyes, and added, "You will walk in here soon feeling that it's all going to be okay. I promise."

It was not the pep talk I was expecting, nor the words that my mind was sober enough to accept. I stopped breathing, clenched my right fist, and squeezed my jaw. I let my head fall and stared at the floor while the words hung in the air. She waited for us to take it all in. After my lungs filled with oxygen again, I unclenched my fist, held my head back up and thanked the oncologist, stood up and guided Ariana out of the door.

We walked out of the office and to the car. We didn't speak the whole way home. I did my best to focus on the road, but I could only think about numbers and try to will the universe to give Ariana 25 years. To let her see her kids graduate and become adults, but the reality sank in the closer we got to home. We knew we only had the next handful of years to live the 30 years we had planned for.

Two weeks later, we were back at the oncologist's office, sitting in the same chairs, squeezed between the same examination table, talking to the oncologist, and everything was "okay."

We eventually moved back home after Ariana's initial treatment and for the next five-and-a-half years we spent every moment we could, trying to be as normal as possible and making as many memories as we could. In those five years, we would spend every three months, sitting in hospitals while she got scanned and then waiting for the call with the results. Most times it was bad news: "The cancer has spread. We need to try something else."

It was a slow descent into the darkness as each new progression of her disease required us to make adjustments to our lives and learn to live with her cancer. Step by step, it diminished the light from our world. People often think grief begins at the moment of loss, but it starts long before that. Anticipatory grief is real and it is a destructive force if surrendered to it.

Ariana grounded us in the truth–we were not special, and the same thing was happening thousands of times over every day around the world. We held on to that belief as we lived our remaining years together. I had found it a struggle to find community and people who understood what I was feeling while caring for Ariana. When she died on September 30, 2020, during a worldwide pandemic, that struggle only intensified. I was alone. Alone in my thoughts, in my words, in my feelings and in my life. My voice extinguished and I had died with Ariana.

The year that followed her death was a season of identity crisis and waking up every day quite literally unsure if I would make it back to my bed. It was difficult to describe that to people around me. The constant gnawing at my heart and pushing me to the edge of my ability to continue.

Yet despite it, I arrogantly went into my loss proclaiming–internally–that I would be the best griever to ever live. I would do all the therapies and my grief would have no hold on me. What really happened was initiation after initiation into the depth of pain and suffering as I confronted each and every thing my grief wanted to show me.

It took fall after fall, bruises and scraped knees, questioning every assumption that surfaced until I was finally able to admit that I had no control over my grief. I so desperately wanted to control it but it is a free-range emotion with no master. And while I knew grief was a life sentence, I still found myself confronted with processing how different my reality was versus the myths I was expecting.

We shield ourselves from death and refuse to talk about it. We keep it contained and hidden away in hospitals, therapist offices, and even inside our bodies. As a result, we have developed strongly held myths about what grief really is. I spent so much time questioning what I was experiencing and comparing my reality to the reality I believed I should be experiencing. This led to a deeply held belief that something was fundamentally wrong with me. I let the myths and societal expectations determine my sanity.

WHAT LIES IN GRIEF

So many persuasive myths about grief have infected our world and as a result, are creating more suffering than is necessary during the toughest moments of our lives. Let me start with the one that frustrates me the most: "Grief follows a set of stages." It doesn't. It really doesn't. The research conducted by Dr. Elisabeth Kübler-Ross back in 1969 was primarily conducted with dying patients confronting their mortality. While the 'stages of grief' were later applied to other types of grief, they were never intended to be a natural law or even a reality in every single person. So, I might experience a different subset of the stages than you. There is no "working through each stage."

Grief is wholly personal and will present the way it wants to present.

If I'm honest, when people would confront me with it and ask or imply I need to work through "the next stage," I would become enraged. I felt like it reduced my experience to a series of logical next steps.

Which leads me to "time heals all wounds" and the mythology we have created around the sentiment. I experienced expectations of work and culture that it was time to be "past my grief." It bred deep resentment and anger in me towards others. Because, while time can provide perspective and distance, it does not erase the pain of loss. Grief isn't something to be "fixed" or "cured"; healing is about cultivating a growing relationship with it. It is a part of who you are, and it will continue to shape your life in ways both big and small.

Grief is not just an emotional experience; it is very much a physical one as well. It profoundly impacts your physical health, often manifesting as fatigue, changes in appetite, and difficulty sleeping. It will also weaken your immune system. The first year, I slept on average 3.5 hours a night. For an entire year! I would end up sick for months on end. So sick, I struggled to function and often had to stay in bed. And yet, I had no choice but to keep going. Bills had to be paid. Kids had to be fed and life had to keep moving, despite everything in my body screaming to stop.

The early days of grief are overwhelming. The initial shock of loss is disorienting and you might even question every belief and meaning of your life. It was hard for my mind and nervous system to adapt to the enormity of the emotions running through me. I was riddled with guilt that I was the one who survived. I was consistently asking myself *Why me? The kids would be better off with Ariana and without me.* It is important to give ourselves permission to feel whatever emotions arise, without judgment or expectation. The more we ignore them or avoid them, the stronger they become. We cannot outrun grief.

Your support systems may disintegrate as new ones are built. I had a difficult time being around people who knew me as Ariana's husband. I, subconsciously, found myself distancing from my family and friends and finding new groups of people who didn't know my past.

And self-care could look as simple as getting out of bed, eating and going to sleep. There is no overstating just how insidious grief is to our physical minds and bodies. It took time for me to accept my limitations and be willing to forgo the life I had before Ariana died. I had to adjust my routines and create new ones. I had to look at myself with sobriety and create new beliefs.

WHY I WROTE THIS BOOK

What follows in this book might seem like the rantings of a madman but I assure you they are not. They are simply a grief-stricken brain that was trying to understand and wrap its head around how to get his future back and to move forward and build a new world for himself and his kids.

The journey of this book has been years in the making, starting the moment I found out Ariana had cancer. The words themselves were written in the first year after her death, but the thoughts and feelings were quietly building beneath the surface. This book is not just a collection of words and sketches; it is a testament to the evolution of grief, a mirror reflecting the shattered pieces of a life once whole and the slow and painful process of reassembling them into something new.

The collection of stories in this book were not written first for an audience, but for myself. They were my lifeline, a way to process the unimaginable, to make sense of the chaos that was consuming my world: raw, unfiltered, and unapologetically honest. They were my way of holding on, of documenting the pain, the anger, the confusion, and the love that refused to die even as she did.

A year and a half after I finished these entries, the idea for this book took shape. It was born out of a need to package up all those fragmented thoughts, to create something tangible out of the intangible. The first version of the book came together quickly, fueled by a sense of urgency and a desire to show the world what grief really looks like. It was a way to say, *this is what it feels like to lose someone you love. This is what it feels like to be broken and it's okay to feel this way. It's okay to be broken.*

Grief is not something we talk about openly. It's not something we share in everyday conversation. We tiptoe around it, afraid to name it, afraid to acknowledge its presence. And when we do experience it, we often feel like we're going insane. We question if we are wrong for feeling a certain way and struggle to know what is normal.

The truth is, grief is messy. It's complicated. It's full of contradictions. Contradictions like "Widow's Fire." For the uninitiated, Widow's Fire is this insatiable pull for physical touch and sex right after you lose your partner. I had heard about it before Ariana passed, but experiencing it is something entirely different. To be broken by your loss and at the same time have this intense, almost primal urge to be intimate with someone else while you still mourn the loss of the person you loved most in the world. It's a duality that's challenging to reconcile—the person you love is gone, and yet all you want is to be close to someone else.

It can be easy to understand that our minds and hearts just want to feel closeness after that deep connection with our person has been severed. My nervous system, mind, and body were all searching for safety, comfort, and a sense of being cared for. But when you are in the midst of it, it can be devastating to navigate.

These are all the things that are not talked about, and the painful reality of learning how to move forward when the future is non-existent. A void. There is nothing in the mind's eye but darkness. Grief breaks you. It shatters your identity, your sense of self, and leaves you in a place of complete isolation. You wake up each day wondering if you'll survive it. There's no guarantee. And yet, you have to find your way through it. There is no choice, really.

People will ask if you're okay, but often what they are really asking is, *are you back to who you used to be?* And the truth is, you're not. You'll never be that person again. You're something new, an infant learning to navigate a world that feels foreign. So, you're left standing there, blank-faced, trying to explain that you're not the same—that you can't be treated the same.

I've interviewed so many people, and not one has been able to escape their grief. You could spend months or years numbing and avoiding but it will eventually catch up to you. And avoiding differs for each of us, but be honest with yourself, you know what you do when you are avoiding the discomfort and pain.

WHAT YOU WILL FIND INSIDE

Stepping into the path with grief is stepping into a path filled with shards of glass. At first, your feet are soft, and every step is agony. You sit down, rest, maybe someone sits with you, but the pain is still there. Soon, you have to get up and keep walking. Over time, your feet callous. The glass is still there, embedded in your skin, but you can walk faster, with more intention. Eventually, you can look up and see the path ahead. To begin to make out the shapes and details of what might lie ahead on the path.

This book is my journey through that broken glass. It's the intimate account of my first year. My hope is for you to feel seen, to know that it's okay to be broken, and to give you permission to feel with no self-judgment. I have made countless mistakes in my life, and specifically in the past four years since losing Ariana.

I have been negligent with my family and friends. I have been overly harsh, overbearing, but also dismissive and distant from my children. I have believed many lies about myself and my life. Yet, worst of all, I have used my grief as an excuse for all of it.

Vulnerability is everything. Without it, we can't confront our grief, our shadows, the parts of us that hurt to be seen. It's the only way to come out the other side. It's the only solution I have found to every wrongdoing I have ever done. To make myself vulnerable in my failings and in my wins. To be willing to look within at my bias, judgments, and harsh criticisms.

This book is only one person's experience navigating the life-changing effects of grief and despair. I am a deeply flawed human. And for all the self-awareness I have cultivated, it feels like there is so much more to go.

So don't take these pages as *the* definitive way to grieve– because there is no right way to grieve. There is no timeline, no roadmap, no set of rules to follow. Grief is deeply personal, and it looks different for everyone.

Let me repeat: It's okay to feel lost. It's okay to be broken. It's okay to not have all the answers. Grief is not something you "get over." It's something you learn to live with.

MESSAGE TO THE READER

If there is one thing I desperately desire you to walk away with, it is to know you are not alone and that whatever you are experiencing is normal. Grief itself is a tricky beast; it will express itself however it wants, and we have no power over its wreckage upon our hearts and minds. All we can do is accept it as our lifelong companion and let it run its course.

The hard truth is that the longer we avoid it, the harder we push it down, the stronger the explosion will be when it finally surfaces. Please take your time with this book. It is not a chapter book or reference book, but more a splattering of emotions that fell onto the page.

One ask before you begin, please be willing to be honest with yourself. If anything comes up as you are scanning this book, acknowledge it. Be curious about the thoughts that come up, the emotions or sensations you feel in your body, and do your best not to run away.

This is my story, but it is yours too. If you are willing, let's walk this path together.

Thank you, again, dear reader, for being here. It means more than you will ever know to me that you choose to spend your time, energy, and money on this.

- CJ Infantino

PART 1:
BEGINNINGS

OUR BEGINNING

Feburary 9, 2003

I paused for a moment, mid-bite. My eyes froze on Ariana as she spun pasta around her fork, speared a piece of chicken, and then hurried the forkful into her mouth.

Conversation faded after the waitress brought our food. Our small table was pinched between two larger ones; it was difficult to move our chairs in or out. People occasionally bumped into us on their way to the bathroom. But we welcomed the warmth rising from our plates. Outside, it was cold and blustery. The wind threw snow against the windows of the small restaurant. Typical Rochester weather for an atypical Valentine's Day.

"How's the food?" I asked.

"Amazing," Ariana replied, looking up at me, still chewing.

I smiled. Our first date. *She would fit right in at our Sunday dinners. She's not holding back. Digging right into her food.*

"What colleges did you end up applying to?" I asked.

"Uh, RIT, WPI, and Drexel. How about you?"

"Well, none yet. I haven't taken my SATs, and I don't think I'm going to. I heard the community college might let you in without them. So, probably MCC."

The food continued to disappear from our plates. Nearby conversations muffled and faded into white noise. I looked over at Ariana as she soaked up the last bit of sauce with a piece of bread. *Amazing.*

"Do you see the couple to our right? They are definitely fighting right?" I asked.

"Yes! I noticed them too. You can practically feel the tension between them."

"Yea, seriously. It's always so awkward fighting in public."

"Yea, I agree," she said.

"Did you enjoy your food?" I asked.

"Yea, it was really good. You?"

"Yea."

The lights flickered in the restaurant as the snow continued to pile up outside. The waitress walked over and asked if we wanted to see a dessert menu. "Yes, please," Ariana said. Hesitant, I grabbed the menu. *Shit, I don't really eat dessert. I get so strict about eating sugar. But how much of an ass would I look like if she ordered and I skipped?*

"Did you want any dessert or coffee?" I asked.

"Not here," she said. "Nothing looks good. Let's go to The Spot instead?"

"Sure," I said, relieved.

The waitress brought our check. We paid and braced ourselves for the walk to the car. Ariana wore a dress that fell above her knees and had squeezed her feet into a pair of high heels–a choice she was already regretting. The snow refused to stop. The sidewalks were buried. I wrapped her arm in mine and tensed my muscles as we high–stepped our way through the drifts to the car, doing my best to keep her from falling into the snow.

"Ready?" I asked.

"Yeah. Turn the heat on. I'm freezing."

We drove to The Spot. We found a place to park and walked to the entrance. It was a open room two-floor building. Walking in you had a clear view of the second-floor landing. A giant square counter of metal and glass dominated the center of the first floor. It was filled with pies, cakes, cookies, and muffins.

One section was devoted to coffee and hot drinks. We got

in line and waited for our turn. I looked at her, and a fleeting image hit me: *this same line, years later, my hand not squeezing hers, but gripping a small, square box in my pocket.*

"What do you want?" I asked.

"Probably just a coffee. I'm pretty full from dinner. You?"

"Same. I'm probably just going to get a tea. I don't eat dessert." *Idiot. You didn't need to say anything about dessert. She wasn't getting any. You were off the hook.*

It was our turn to order. Ariana ordered her coffee. I got my tea. We made our way up the stairs to the second floor. It was lit by small sconces, casting shadows in every corner. Couches and chairs, worn and torn, were scattered around, mostly filled with intertwined couples.

"Is this, like, retro style, or are these couches just old and nasty?" she asked.

"I think they're just old and nasty, but maybe they're trying to pass it off as vintage."

"Let's sit on the chairs over there. They don't look as gross."

"Yup, you read my mind," I said.

I sat down first. Ariana sat down next to me. A burst of electricity seemed to shoot through my heart; it skipped a beat before settling. The conversation continued. She talked. I sipped my tea. I responded. She sipped her coffee. And so it continued until our drinks ran out. The conversation flowed with ease. No awkward pauses. No uncomfortable silence.

"Are you enjoying hanging out?" she asked.

"I am. A lot. How about you?"

"Same."

"Want to head back to your dad's house now?"

"That works."

We left and drove back, carefully navigating the snow-obscured streets.

I pulled into the driveway. The windows looked dark and bare. Moonlight illuminated the driveway but left the inside of the house in shadow. *Is anyone home?*

"You want to come in?" Ariana asked.

"Uh-huh," I said, reaching for the key to turn the engine off.

We got out of the car and headed to the front door. A knot tightened in my stomach, and a warm, clammy feeling flooded my palms despite the chill air. I shoved my hands in my pockets and waited for Ariana to open the door.

"We can hang out over there," she said as we walked into the entryway, pointing to a faded purple couch.

The sofa was smoothed from years of napping and sitting. I took my coat off, laid it on the bench, and sat criss-cross on the couch.

Ariana went into the kitchen. I waited, staring out the window, watching the wind swirl the snow around the yard.

"I got this for you. It's apple!" Ariana said, pushing the plate towards my face.

"What? Oh, man. You didn't have to do that."

I took the plate and looked down. There was a piece of apple pie and a scoop of ice cream. Chunks of apple were falling from the sides of the pie. The ice cream dripped down.

"Are your parents home?" I asked.

"Yeah, they must be in bed already."

I scooped up a piece of pie with my fork, making sure to get some ice cream. I lifted it to my mouth, paused, glanced at Ariana, then at the pie, and finally took a bite. We finished our pie while recounting the evening. I set the fork and the plate down on the floor.

"Wait, didn't you say earlier that you don't eat dessert?" Ariana asked.

"Yeah."

"Hm, but you just ate dessert."

"Yeah." I looked away. "I guess I did." Heat rushed up my neck, warming my cheeks.

I gathered our plates and walked them to the kitchen, setting them in the sink. On my way back, I ducked into the bathroom. Turning on the light, I checked my reflection. My face still normal, not flushed. Good. My chest tightened anyway. I reached for the doorknob, hesitated, then turned back to flush the toilet and wash my hands, stalling.

I walked back to the living room. I sat back down on the couch, still sitting criss-cross. We faced each other.

Her mouth tightened slightly, and her eyes narrowed as she leaned back.

"What's up?" she asked.

"Huh?"

"You're not telling me something."

"What do you mean?"

"I mean, I can tell that you want to tell me something."

She jumped towards me, pushing me back against the couch cushions and pinning my hands. "Tell me!"

"There's nothing to say," I lied, the clammy feeling returning to my palms.

"You're lying. Now tell me," Ariana demanded.

"I mean... okay." My throat swelled.

"Okay, what?" she asked.

"What I wanted to say was, well... I don't know. It was a good night. I'm glad we finally made this happen."

"Yeah, me too," she said.

"I just feel... I don't know... like we've known each other our whole lives, you know? It's hard to explain."

"Yeah, I know what you mean," she said, returning to her spot on the couch. I sat up, relieved. *Will she drop it now?*

"So, anything else?" she asked, her gaze steady on my lips.

"Huh? What else do you want me to say?"

Her eyes narrowed. "I know you want to say it. So just say it." *No. No. I can't do this. She'll think I'm crazy, insane, or just weird and run away.*

"Okay, fine. Ariana. I... well, I think... I think I'm in love with you. I... I love you."

She turned away, hiding her face so I could only see part of her profile. *Was that a smirk? A smile? Shock?* I couldn't tell. Finally, she looked back at me. *Okay, she's grinning. Is that good or bad? What is she thinking? Please just say something. Anything.*

The moment stretched. My words hung heavy in the air, seeming to press against my ribs.

"Ah, okay then," she said slowly. *Okay what? Oh shit, she thinks I'm crazy. It's only our first date. Why would I say that?* "Yeah. You said it. You actually said it," she continued.

She got up from the couch and headed towards the kitchen entryway, then paused and turned back. *What. Is. Going. On?* I stayed frozen on the couch.

Her smirk grew into a full smile. "I love you too."

PART 2:
HOSPICE CARE

IN A MOMENT OF SUPREME CRISIS

CONFESSIONS OF A MALE

With my rock-hard abs and "main character energy," I thought
showered in women's attention. Fifteen years later, I'm burying I lost
BY DANIEL MEH

AYS, I CARRIED MYSELF WITH SWAGGER.
—that's the role I liked to play. But today, I
n the way I used to years ago. These days, I
to mellow my manner in mixed company.
seam, which for decades I had endured w
aims sent me on a quest leading to
ectified women in the world. I
ferent movies, and looked
've figured things out r
gray and I'm still r

and elbows. Plus I rarely asked
of interrupting the answers.
I addressed my girl problem
some of that main character en
clever remarks and told impre
dominat muscles and chogg
rockside. I did all this with the
ng horses with them, ais
s I would've settled fo
o meaningful relati
then. But they d
seemed like a c
all over the

YOUR PAIN

EVERYONE FEELS THE HURT / ___ ___ PUT
'D CAN HELP YOU DEAL W"

lly does fly by. Before I knew it, my 40s
ed, and with them came some new gifts
. of Mother Nature—frequent Arrm
. less energy and sleeple
at about these thim
he young and
'middle-age' r
elp but feel
ind my ani
ae No'
t a b

INVITATION ONLY

HER GOODBYE

september 10, 2020

"It's been a long 5 months on my newest chemo. I had a stable scan 2 months ago with no new growth but no response or shrinking.

We stayed the course and everything seemed to be responding well until about a couple weeks ago when I started holding fluid in my lungs and stomach. I was having similar liver issues as before.

A couple procedures and about 4 scans later I found out that although the cancer in my liver seemed to be shrinking, it was pretty badly damaged from the years of chemo and targeted drugs, I had new growth in my bowel and also 17 spots in my brain. I start full brain radiation Monday and a new chemo next Wed. I get to start steroids and a fun new Alzheimer's drug for my radiation induced short term memory loss. And I switched over to a palliative care team.

To say it's been a whirlwind is a massive understatement. We canceled a large housing project to focus on buying watches for the boys, future birthday presents, cards, recording videos for the kids, updating our estate and affairs and today I picked out my plot and marker.

The kids are devastated, as are we. A lot has changed in such a short time. I started propagating all my plants so that at my funeral everyone can have a small part of my memory and Grace will get to keep the mother plants.

And it was so truly peaceful picking out my plot today. I felt calm and in a good place. I will be next to a swing overlooking a waterfall and stream on one of Whitehaven's ever-wild trails.

Silver linings:
- I'm no longer on a diet, I ate coffee cake and a pack

of double bubble gum the other night for dinner

- All my affairs will be in order so I don't have to have that on my mind
- I won't have to bury my sweet precious dogs and actually they are allowed to visit the cemetery
- I had a sweetened Starbucks refresher lemonade instead of a black coffee, because fuck sugar
- I've been buying some really freaking sweet plants lately
- I have the best family and friends that are hurting and pushing through with us
- Ativan and medicinal marijuana

Pray I make it out of 2020 alive, please don't let me die in this butt eff of a year. I'll even take Jan 1st of 2021. And in the words of Leslie Chow from Hangover, **'Toodaloo motherfuckers!'**

- Ariana Infantino
Wife, Mother, Daughter, Friend, and All Around Badass

I'm not good enough to do this without her.

Day One
09.25.2020

"Hi friends and family.
I wanted to update everyone about Ariana. She has finished radiation but unfortunately her liver is struggling. She has transitioned to hospice care and we are now managing her pain. She sends all her love to you."

Day Two
09.26.2020

"I do not feel strong anymore.
My heart is physically breaking apart.
I am being undone."

Day Five
09.29.2020

"This week has been a beautiful tragedy. I have moved in and out of agony, sadness, and acceptance. This morning I woke up and my heart was skipping, my liver hurt and I had trouble breathing. I got up and ran into the room to check on Ariana. It was dark, the kids were sleeping and I saw her breathe. The symptoms subsided. Since being with Ariana I have always developed sympathy pains with her. I can't explain it, I know it sounds unreal but it happens.

Through her pregnancies, surgeries, and treatments, I felt it all too a much lesser degree. I have been scared to lose that connection with her. It has been torturing me.

I was unable to sleep Friday and Saturday because I felt like I was dying along with her every time I closed my eyes. But now that I can sleep, my mind is consumed with another fear–I wasn't good enough to her. I fear I didn't thank her enough for how amazing she made my life and my kids life. I am broken that I didn't do enough for her during her time with this fucking disease. I know some of you may say it's absurd or irrational, but it's hard to not look back and find moments where I could have been better.

She deserved the world, the moon and the sun. And I worry I only gave her the world."

Final Day
09.30.2020 - 11:08AM

"The unknown is now known. My best friend is finally at rest. My heart is physically broken but our love will transcend time and space. I will carry her with me, always."

PART 3:
THE FIRST YEAR

It feels like my body and mind are numb...

THE FIRST NIGHT

october 01, 2020

The daytime distractions quieted down, and the house became still. Everything I saw and touched reminded me of her. The placement of her toothbrush, purse, and shoes–all the everyday things around the house–sat frozen in their places.

It was the last time she had touched any of them. I wondered what she thought or felt as she put them down in their final resting places. Her death was the longest shortest journey. It felt long and pained but ended so fast and abrupt.

It really hit home when I tucked the kids into my bed. I turned the TV on. I wanted to give them a distraction to help them fall asleep. It was the last show we watched with Mommy on that same bed. We cried together and remembered Ariana. We recognized the loss we had taken. I remembered that I am a single-widowed parent. I reassured them that we would endure this pain.

I remained with the kids until they all fell asleep. Afterwards, I went downstairs and tried to do normal things like watching TV and talking with my sister. I kept waiting for Ariana to come into the room with us. I kept waiting for her to laugh at one of my jokes. I grew tired of waiting and decided to go to bed.

I closed my eyes and eventually fell asleep. Everything felt normal in my dream. It was the standard self-deprecating type of dream–I was doing something wrong; it needed to be rectified. When the main story of my dream ended, my eyes opened. I'd had a full night's sleep, but woke to my new reality; she was no longer with me.

HER SMILE

october 02, 2020

My hand ached from holding the phone. I couldn't find the sweet spot between being comfortable in bed and seeing the screen. This was unlike me – screen time before bed, or more accurately, screen time instead of sleep. I turned over and let the phone rest on the bed. My arm fell into position, resting on my side, with my hand barely touching the phone, just enough to keep it from falling.

I had no particular intention or purpose except to distract myself. Honestly, I think I was just waiting for sleep to find me, and I couldn't do anything except scroll. I felt nothing and everything. My mind was reeling; it was hard to even comprehend the thoughts and images in my head.

One swipe of my thumb and my photos appeared. The "photo of the day" filled the rectangular glass screen. An image of Ariana and me. We were in some nondescript location. White walls. My right arm extended in the left part of the frame holding the phone. The other arm pulled Ariana close to me. Our heads filled the frame.

After her diagnosis, I made it a point to document as much of our lives together as possible. I had hundreds of selfies of us; the same pose, different locations. My eyes were fixed on her. I noticed her smile was big and vibrant.

I continued scrolling through our photos, noticing she always seemed to be smiling. I started to question how much pain her smile was hiding. How much was happening inside her that I didn't even notice – or more honestly, couldn't bring myself to accept? I was too scared in that photo, just as I was too scared now.

I closed my eyes and tried to bring myself back to that place and time. I did my best to smile back, but I could only think about my failure to notice Ariana's pain. I told myself I did the best I could, but it wasn't enough. The guilt, anger, fear, and brokenness took over.

My mind twisted.

Was she hurting all those nights she was slow to come upstairs and say goodnight to the kids? Was her phone a distraction for her, a numbing agent? Like it has become for me? If so, why did I get frustrated with her when she was on it? When I was impatient with her, was she acting out due to her disease? What about when I thought only of my hurt or anxiety and demanded she listens to me? Did she do it all despite the abject suffering she was enduring?

My hands reached for my chest, grabbing hold of my shirt. They pulled at the fabric and beat against my ribs until the skin turned red. I clenched my eyes tighter and cried out to Ariana.

"I'm sorry. I'm so fucking sorry for not giving you more. I'm sorry for all the big and small ways I failed you. And I'm sorry I wasn't stronger, and for all the suffering you had to endure. I'm so, so sorry, Ariana."

I opened my eyes.

Wiped them dry.

I threw my phone off the bed and stared at the ceiling until I finally fell asleep.

My heart is beyond
repair...

"Pain is a universal language. Each and every one of us is in pain for one reason or another. It is not to be feared or avoided. We need to embrace it and share it with others.

We need to be the best versions of ourselves and have enough resilience to lift up others around us. To be strong for the weak. To amplify the voice of the oppressed. We need to stop trying to protect ourselves and trying to preserve our image. Life is not a zero-sum game.

Life can be boiled down to one thing — Love."

— Sep 2, 2020 2:10 PM

THE NEWS

october 04, 2020

Family honors mother's breast cancer fight

Dan Schrack Sat, October 3rd 2020 at 11:17 PM

Penfield, N.Y. — Three days after Ariana Infantino lost her battle with breast cancer, her husband, CJ, said that even in death, the way she lived her life is impacting many.

"The only way I can describe her life is that it burned red hot and died quickly," said Infantino.

Ariana's battle with breast cancer began in 2015 when she was diagnosed with stage 4 metastatic disease.

The high school sweethearts had three children together, including 12-year-old Grace. "I always loved doing art," said Grace, "and my mom was very good at doing it."

About a year ago, at her father's suggestion, Grace started Mossy Inc., a clothing company featuring her drawings of Inky and Georgia, the family's two French Bulldogs.

"I would say about two weeks ago, I spoke to my daughter and I was like, 'Hey, do you want to do something for Breast Cancer Awareness Month? Which is coming up in October,'" Infantino recalled.

Rushing to get the design done in time, Grace said that for her mom, this needed to be perfect.

"So, some of them just come to my mind and it's easy to do," said Grace. "But with the breast cancer one, it was very hard because I felt like I needed it to be perfect. I felt like if it wasn't, it just wouldn't be good."

Grace did get the design done and even showed it to her mother just days before she died. Since its release, the family has seen an outpouring of support.

CJ calls it a ripple effect of a life lived to the fullest.

"The most amazing thing about her is even in her death, she is still pouring into this family — because of all the foundation that she laid and all the seeds that she planted with all of the people that she touched," said CJ. The love and the support that is being poured into this family is unbelievable, and it's undeniably her."

The news report continued on the screen. Ariana's face, larger than life, appeared in photos shown between segments of Grace and me talking. I didn't move, breathe, or blink.

Minutes later, the report cut to commercial. I forced my jaw closed. Wiped my face and looked around the living room.

It was filled with smiles, and the words "Good job, guys!" echoed in the space. It was hard to believe that only four days ago I watched my wife exit this world only to see her return on the TV screen.

I felt a kind of honor, though that doesn't feel quite like the right word. Shock, maybe? But really, how could she *not* be on the news?

She was, after all, a woman worth tribute. She was all that was good in this family, and even in death, she continues to watch over us. Her work, her legacy, and her love live on.

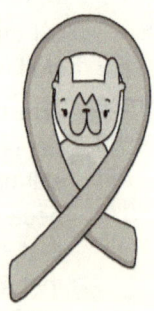

Ariana was born in Seoul, Korea on December 23, 1984. She came to America on May 4th at 4 months old which she celebrated every year as Airplane Day. She fiercely loved her kids and her family. She had a love for Christmas; a passion for baking, eating, cooking and making a home for her family. She traveled the world. She was epitome of strength and will be deeply missed by all.

MUSE DEATH

october 05, 2020

The kids went apple picking yesterday, and for the first time since, I had quiet in my home. The stillness was haunting. Empty really. No matter what room I was in or where I sat, she wasn't there. She was gone. The void felt so profound.

It unnerved me.

I planned to sit down and finally tackle the eulogy, but I watched TV with my sister instead. It wasn't procrastination, pain, or hurt that kept me from writing; it was my inability to find words to describe who and what Ariana was to me and to this world. How do you sum up someone's life, however short, in fifteen hundred words? What justice is that to their legacy and the love they poured into all they met? The challenge felt too enormous and overwhelming. I didn't want to let Ariana down.

Not again.

So today, I promised myself I would write. I would chip away at my insecurities, word by word, until I found the right words, the right sentences, the right sentiment. I got up, sat down at the table, opened my laptop, and wrote this instead.

"*I have time,*" I told myself, but I knew I was lying. *Is it possible my Muse died along with Ariana? Was Ariana my Muse? Or is it that my mind has gone numb to protect itself?* All questions I used to distract myself, to keep from writing the eulogy

So, I guess we'll find out Saturday if my Muse is alive and well when I get up to speak.

FAMILIA JEALOUSY

october 07, 2020

I reached over Cam and grabbed the TV remote from the nightstand. I had little space to move, squeezed in between all the kids. I clicked the remote, and the TV lit up the room. The show started. There was no arguing or complaining about what to watch.

No comments. No questions.

Just silence.

It was unsettling.

Two minutes into the show, I realized it was the first time we had watched it since Ariana died. What used to be a nightly show that brought us together in laughter was now just something to numb our minds. I watched the story unfold, doing my best to pay attention. Suddenly, my stomach clenched. My fists formed. Jealousy surfaced. There they were, a "complete" family running around on my TV screen.

Mocking me. Mocking us.

Showing us what we used to have, what our lives used to be.

And now, we were a family of four. My mind had yet to fully comprehend that and to truly understand what it meant to no longer be "Ariana and CJ." Who was I, what was I, after having half my soul ripped from me?

The night before, I had sat around a table listening to stories told about Ariana through her friends' eyes. It was beautiful and bitter, hearing who she was to them, hearing stories of the woman I once shared my life with. My face smiled some; my heart did not. I desperately wanted to laugh with Ariana again and let her know that I loved her one more time.

And so, the show carried on. The fictional family made it through their adventure. The kids' eyes drifted closed, and they fell asleep. I turned off the TV, tossed the remote aside, and shut my eyes.

I replaced the jealous thoughts with anxious ones about finishing the eulogy. I prayed my Muse would come quickly and that her words would pour into me. The funeral was three days away. I begged my Muse to hold back my tears so I could read the eulogy uninterrupted. Hour by hour, I was learning how to carry grief forward. I recognized that it might look different for me than someone else, which was okay. I needed to stop placing judgments on my journey. It was my journey and mine alone. I had to accept whatever my path may be.

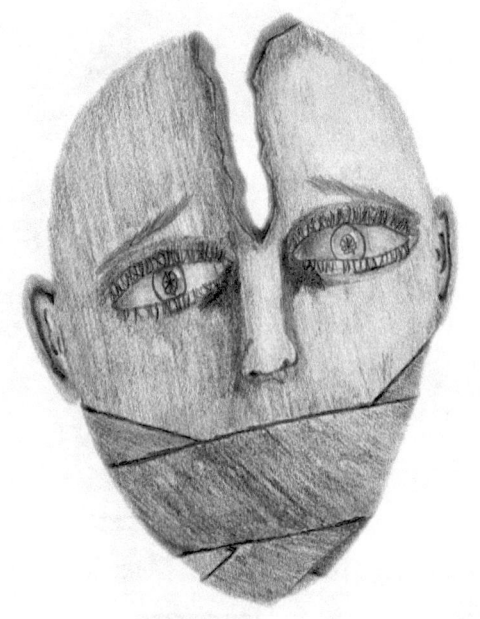

"I am my unraveling. In each situation, in everyday moments, I feel I am living as two people.
One is the man who still has a wife, working together with her.
The other is the man imagining being alone. Raising his kids, alone."

— Aug 24, 2020 8:34 AM

THE EULOGY

october 10, 2020

This was the most challenging thing to write, not because of the context but because of the subject. There are no words I could use that would properly describe who and what Ariana was to me, to my kids, to her friends and family. There are no adjectives strong enough to describe the pain of my soul being rendered as I watched my best friend slowly fade away.

I have seen Ariana through many different eyes these past few weeks, and only now realize how deeply she impacted others. It was hard to see that when my own eyes were always the ones looking upon her.

Back in 2016, Ariana had finished her initial treatment. The chemo was done; her surgeries were healed. We had made it through one of the most difficult years, and to celebrate, we took a trip to Asia with our friends.

It was halfway through our trip when we found ourselves alone, sitting on the floor of the apartment we rented in Japan. The room was dark and still. Ariana turned to me and broke the silence, telling me how happy she was to be in Asia, how lucky she felt, and how grateful she was for the time we were spending together. My heart began to swell. I smiled and told her that I loved her.

She paused, and her eyes fell to the floor. Her smile faded, and the energy in the room changed. She looked back at me and told me that she got a call before leaving for our trip. Her cancer was back. My heart started to race, and my palms began to sweat. I was heartbroken all over again. Ariana let the moment hang in the air and gave me space to process. She started laughing a few moments later and told me she was just kidding.

That set the tone for her entire battle with cancer.

For Ariana, everything in life was to be enjoyed, laughed at, or loved. There was little room for anything else. She gave generously and intensely protected those who were close to her. She was my best friend.

A few months ago, when we got the news that the cancer had spread to her brain, she asked me if I thought I was winning or losing at life. I paused to think.

Ariana and I knew we were not special, just two people out of seven billion on this earth. Suffering was all around us; we were not alone. So there was no reason to be angry about what was happening.

Ariana taught me how to love unconditionally, live freely, and defend passionately over the nearly two decades we were together. The lessons were often painful and difficult, but our love was forged in that fire. We grew into adults together, and our spirits became one.

Over the years, the battle for her life was a continuous breaking of my heart, mind, and soul. In the final week of her life, my own physical pain felt unbearable as our spirits became untethered. Yet, it was the least I could do for her. The pain I carried and endured was not comparable to the pain she held onto and safeguarded.

Ariana could love in the worst of times and showed me how to be there for others, even when I didn't want to be. During my depression, she stood by my side, despite the pain it caused her. She showed me how to care for someone in need. She prepared me, unknowingly, to be there for her during her six years living with cancer.

Ariana was all in when she committed. Whether it was parties, holidays, or spending, she never held back. She paid attention to others and always knew the perfect gift to give. She taught me that it was okay to enjoy material possessions, big or small.

She could be equally lazy and do nothing for long stretches. She never apologized for it or felt bad. She taught me that life wasn't always about "doing." A lesson that I am still learning.

Ariana refused to stand down when someone she loved was being attacked. She would burn with rage against those who dared hurt her kids, family, or friends. It was a form of love I could never replicate. She was my protector.

Our story has ended; it is complete. In the short time we were together, we experienced life in full. We traveled the world. We were near divorce. We fought. We loved. She saw me through my depression. I got to care for her until death. We were inseparable. We did nearly everything we set out to do, except grow old together.

So, when she asked if I thought I was winning at life, it wasn't hard to answer yes. I have felt pain and loneliness to degrees I never imagined, and I have fought for a love more profound than I ever thought possible. And I got to do it all with the most incredible friend who ever came into my life.

I know many of you feel the pain in your hearts right now; I want you to know it's okay. We are going to be okay. All of us. Me, the kids, and all of you.

The pain that Ariana suffered was incomprehensible. And when she broke, in the quiet of the night, with just the two of us, it was made clear how much she had taken on herself.

Despite all of it, her death has also truly been a celebration of her life. And that is exactly what she would have wanted.

Her life burned red hot, then faded quickly. She lived with an unwavering passion and a relentless pursuit of life. She taught us all what we needed to know. In your sadness, find her lessons. In your happiness, enjoy as she would enjoy. Love fiercely. Defend others unapologetically. And let everything else go.

She has given us the example of how to live a life fully, despite it being filled with pain and sorrow.

Let your hearts be sad for our loss, but always remember that she is finally at rest. And never forget her parting words to us — "Toodaloo motherfuckers."

Ariana, I will love you until the day I die.

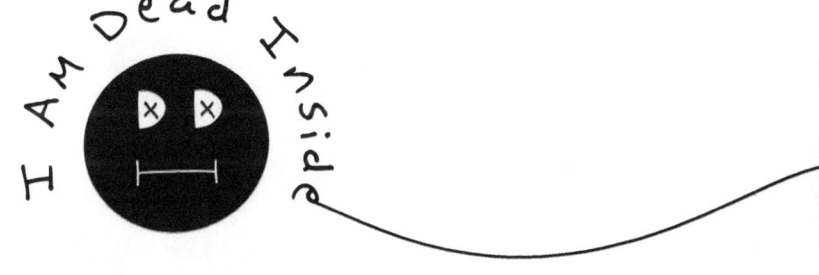

OUR FINAL GOODBYE

october 11, 2020

My sister passed out markers and balloons. We wrote our love notes to Ariana, scribbling all over them. "Ready? One, two, three... go!" I shouted. We released the balloons. They floated up and faded into the skyline.

It was meant as a gesture of closure, a ritual to help ease the heart, yet a large part of me wanted so badly to believe Ariana would somehow see the balloons. I imagined her catching them, reading our final goodbyes. I wanted her to smile because of me one more time. Then a conflicting thought came: how painful it might be for her to read our broken words. I pictured her weeping, her tears falling onto the balloons, smudging the marker, losing our words forever.

"C'mon," my friend said, gesturing to us. I shook the images from my head and followed him. He carried a large flower arrangement from the funeral down onto the pier. The wind whipped cold droplets of water into our faces. The further down the pier we went, the harder and more frequently we were hit. Arriving near the end, my friend flung the flowers into the lake. A Viking funeral, sorta.

And then we waited for the water to swallow the flowers and push them out beyond our eyeline. We waited. And waited. Nothing happened. The waves pushed, but the flowers remained, bobbing stubbornly. Not swallowed. Not moving. When our faces had taken enough of the cold fall air, we ran back to shore.

The day was beautiful; the sendoff was meaningful. It felt like the ideal way to celebrate her life. I felt full, content even. I had seen the love she gave returned to her and her family. So, out of tears and energy, we all went to our cars and left.

I headed home, tired and I fell asleep with a smile on my

face, only to wake up to a very different morning.

Moments after waking, I was overwhelmed with hopelessness and brokenness. My heart yearned for my best friend. My breathing stumbled as I began whispering our song. My mind soaked in memories of when we were young: playful, carefree, whole.

"Thank you, Ariana. For everything. And thank you for this moment, for allowing me to share in your pain. Today, I feel so unbelievably alone. I don't want to be alone. And I hate myself for it. For all of it."

I felt weak, pathetic, stupid. Not too long ago, Ariana and I had talked about her death and what my life would be after she was gone.

"I want you to move on, CJ. I don't want you to be alone. You should be with someone after I'm gone," she told me.

"I can't. How could I? I don't even want to think about it."

"You need to find someone. I don't care who it is; I just want you to be okay moving on. CJ, I can help you find someone if you want."

"What? Are you fucking kidding me? No," I said, nauseated, holding my stomach.

But that is who she was. Always thinking of me. Always thinking of others. She was my protector and my giver. I don't know who I am without her, but I feel okay knowing she left the best parts of herself in me.

So, I continue on, moving forward in my grief.

Hidden Places

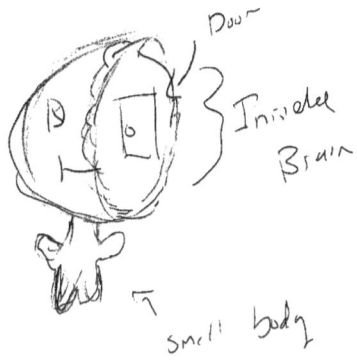

Door

Invisible
Brain

small body

"... It's hard to work through tear soaked eyes.
Everyday is on repeat. I wake up, try
to convince myself to get up, put feet to floor
and tell myself today will be different.
I will Be Productive. I will Make it
through. And it always ends the same.
Defeated. Exhausted. Overwhelmed..."

                          – JAN 20, 2021 6:16 PM

W.I.P.

HER FINAL BREATH

october 16, 2020

Ariana's final moments will not stop tormenting me. They play on loop in my head.

Cool air blew in through the window. The family was seated around her bedside. My nephew was shoving tissues between his eyes and his glasses because apparently, that is what one does when one cannot stop crying.

I sat on the ground, my hand wrapped in hers. I looked up at her and watched, counting the seconds between each breath. Her jaw clenched. Then a shallow breath. She clenched again, and then, nothing. She was gone.

For the past two weeks, I'd felt her presence so strongly. I'd felt her peace. Although peace isn't quite the right word. And now words, once objects of my desire, seem almost irrelevant. I used to find joy in stringing them together, finding the right syntax to emphasize what I was feeling.

But what I feel now is inexpressible.

And no, it's not negative. It's not positive either. It just is. My connection to Ariana has changed. It's there, perhaps, but it's more distant now. It feels like she's nudging me forward, telling me it's okay, reassuring me that she is alright and that I need to move forward in my life.

I love her for that. I'll always love her.

So I'm trying. I'm trying to move forward–in whatever capacity that means–I am trying..

LOST AT SEA

october 18, 2020

My bed is too big for one.

Where I used to sink in, comforted by her presence, my body now floats on the mattress, adrift at sea. There is no longer a body to hold, no longer boundaries to respect. My knees go where they please.

The room is dark and silent. No more glow from her screen. No more late-night laughter.

Tonight, I closed my eyes and summoned her spirit. In my mind, we danced under the light of the stars, and I remembered us. But when my eyes opened, she was gone. It was just me.

This energy, this love I have for her, has no place to go. So it stays bottled up inside, building into a tight ball just beneath my heart. I worry what will happen if it never finds release.

The sun rises and sets twice each day. The moon crests and blooms in a week.

It's not the agony of the present that bothers me; it's the preoccupation with the future.

Will I live to be eighty, dancing under the light of the stars, alone with just her spirit?

And when will my bed stop feeling like a punishment? When will the night bring comfort and peace?

THE FIRST DAY BACK AT SCHOOL

october 20, 2020

Light bled through the crack under my door, hitting my eyes and waking me. I blinked, my eyes gritty as if filled with sand. It had been another night of horrible sleep, but this time, staying up late had been my choice.

I got up and walked out of the bedroom. I looked downstairs, saw my daughter and youngest son sitting at the counter eating breakfast. I walked down the stairs and joined them.

I reminded them that it was Breast Cancer Awareness week at school. I reassured them it was okay to leave the classroom if they needed a minute, telling them I would pick them up immediately if they needed to come home.

What a week to be back at school after your mom just died from breast cancer. Thanks, coincidence.

The kitchen was relatively calm. The kids were laughing, food was being eaten and things were happening. I felt a rush of pride, a hint of okay-ness. I smirked and thought, *"I'm crushing this solo-parent life. Forget the haters."* If I could have seen my reflection then, I undoubtedly would have winked at myself.

A couple of minutes later, I walked my daughter to the front door, kissed her goodbye, and closed it behind her. Two kids left to get ready. I admit, I was looking forward to having the day to myself.

I walked back to the kitchen. The boys were wrestling on the floor. Dishes were still piled on the counter. Crumbs were everywhere.

My blood started to boil. My brain felt like it was beating against my skull. I clenched my fists. The realization hit me: it was just me now. There was no escape valve, no partner to share the load. It was just me, all the time, maybe forever.

I was alone.

My anger, fear, and frustration turned towards my boys.

I screamed at them.

I pounded the counter.

I said things that demeaned them.

I broke down.

It was the first time I had yelled like that since Ariana passed. I walked away into the other room and began yelling at Ariana under my breath: *"How could you leave me? Why did you do this to me? I need you. Please, just come back."* I felt like the full-time bad guy now. There was no one else to share the burden.

The boys' ride showed up. They left, carrying my shame with them into their first day back at school. I went upstairs, crawled into bed, and begged Ariana silently to say something, anything. My eyes closed as I tried to sleep the shame away.

The day proceeded somehow. The kids came home, and we ate dinner. Not a word was spoken about the morning. Later, I tucked them in and went to my room.

I ran a bath for the first time since Ariana's funeral. It used to be my weekly ritual; some nights, if Ariana was feeling okay, she would climb in with me.

I lit the candles. They were the last gift she had bought me. I slowly eased myself into the tub. The water was hot, burning almost, not my preference, but how Ariana liked it.

I sank deeper, letting the water burn my skin. It was painful, but a welcome break from the sadness. I imagined Ariana's shadow across from me, peeking over her phone, smiling. I let my shoulders drop further and the water overtake my face.

My phone buzzed. I grabbed it and saw a text from my friend. I replied briefly, but texting felt too difficult, so I called him for a video chat. *(Oh, it's not weird; we're close. No, really, it's okay; we met on Twitter. Our friendship is totally legit. For real.)*

For the next hour, we told stories about our friendship. We talked about the beginning of Ariana's diagnosis. He reminded me what it was like for him, walking me through it all.

I smiled. I laughed and for a little while, I forgot I was alone.

I released the drain and let the bath empty. I dried off, climbed into bed, and said goodnight to my friend.

I put my phone away, turned to my left—to her empty side of the bed—and said goodnight to Ariana

I smiled, cried, and fell asleep.

"... solo parenthood was not a slow burn but a fast-burning ember that lit quickly and demanded my full attention. Maintaining the house, the kids, school, work, and any sort of personal life has become an always-losing battle.

I feel I have lost myself completely in my responsibilities. The plates are spinning, teetering, and some are on their way to the floor. I never had a chance to learn how to juggle. It truly is a trial by fire.

I'm late. All the time. I'm running around in circles in the house, never sure what to tackle first. Running from chore to work, back to chore, back to work.

My forcefield and defenses — they are all down..."

                              — Jan 20, 2020 6:16 PM

"To measure love's worthlessness by its brevity
Is to measure life's worth by its longevity"

- blonote, Tablo

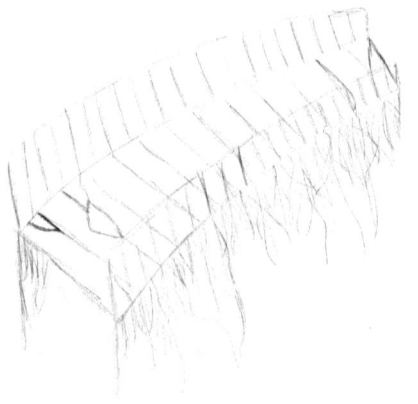

MY HEART

october 25, 2020

My heart has been broken and mended, on repeat, for the last

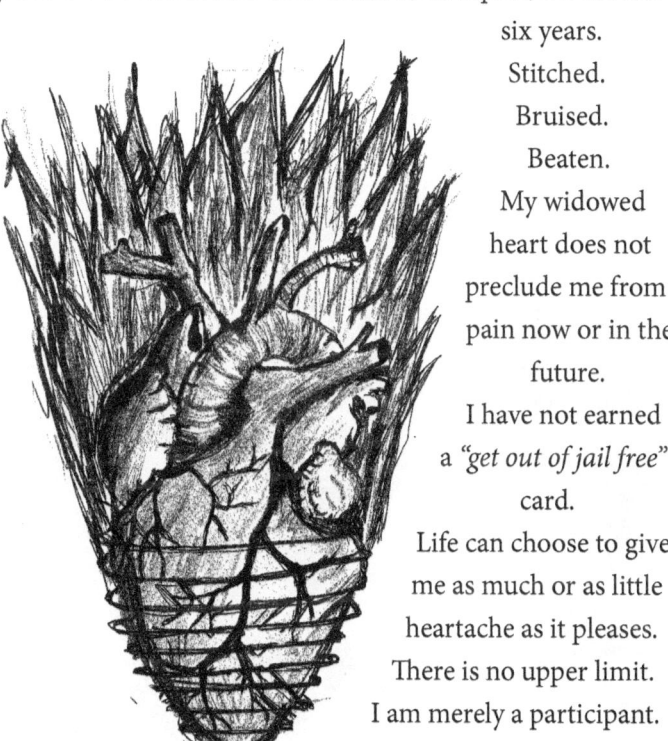

six years.
Stitched.
Bruised.
Beaten.
My widowed
heart does not
preclude me from
pain now or in the
future.
I have not earned
a *"get out of jail free"*
card.
Life can choose to give
me as much or as little
heartache as it pleases.
There is no upper limit.
I am merely a participant.

A HARD CONVERSATION

october 30, 2020

I'm angry, annoyed, and frustrated.

With you.

Please stop projecting your grief and your preconceived ideas of grief onto my kids and me.

Please stop being surprised when I'm holding it together, keeping the kids fed, keeping the house clean, as if this is suddenly new for me. Who do you think took care of things when Ariana was sick or recovering from procedures?

Why does it feel like the standards are lower for me? As if the expectations would be much higher if I were a woman?

Listen—hear me out—you were not here for the past six years. You do not know what we went through day in and day out. You don't understand what our journey was or what it is now. You do not know my needs: not what they have been, nor what they will be.

If you genuinely want to be there for my kids and me, then you will not judge our actions, laughter, tears, or decisions. If you truly believe that each person has their own journey to walk, then you will believe us when we say we are doing what is right for us.

Unsolicited advice feels like judgment. I can feel your pity, and it only isolates me further. I get to choose what is right for my kids and me. I get to choose who I want to be around. I get to decide how I deal with my loss. Not you.

But also remember.

I still love you.

Even if you anger me.

"These are lyrics from a song I carried with me for five years — anticipating the day I would lose Ariana. Today was the first day I listened to it since her passing."

— oct 30, 2020

"[...] This night is pulling on my heart's strings,
These feelings bring tears to my eyes
To see you leave my world
Leave my side [...]
[...] Tomorrow,
The air will be a little colder
But I'll be sure to breathe for the both of us.
And the nights
May be a little darker
But I'll be sure to carry the torch to warm the hearts that never
got to feel yours
I can't hear your voice
I can't hear your voice
But that's OK
'Cause I can feel you in my heart [...]"

- Beauty In Tragedy, August Burns Red

OUR TREE

November 10, 2020

I reached into the bin for another ornament. I grabbed one, pulled it out, and unwrapped it from wrinkled tissue paper. Written on its face was "Our First Christmas, 2003." My hand tensed, squeezing the small porcelain figurine. My throat tightened, and sobs stuttered out of my body. Tears wet my face. I sank to the ground, letting my head rest against the floor. I yelled and screamed at Ariana, enraged.

"Why was I left alone? Why are my days and nights now void of your laughter and stupidity? Why am I stuck decorating all these fucking Christmas trees? Upholding your traditions?"

I was left to fill her shoes; ones that felt far too big for me.

I beat the floor.

My fists burned and throbbed.

Finally, the sobbing subsided. I took a deep breath and continued decorating our tree. It was small and sat tucked away in front of the windows in our bedroom. I placed each ornament carefully. Each one represented a piece of our life together: ornaments from countries we visited, trips taken with the kids, milestones in our lives.

This cycle of grief, recovery, decorating repeated until the tree was finished.

I live in two states of being now: the old and the new. It is okay; it is normal. This is my new normal, and perhaps this is what it will be for the rest of my life.

This grief, this sadness, this loss—whatever you want to call it—will always be with me. It's not supposed to disappear. It's not something to be "moved on" from. Instead, I will carry it with me into my next chapter. Chapter Two.

I might cry and bang the floor in protest against the loss I have suffered, and in the next moment, be thinking about something else entirely. And yes, perhaps the intense moments of sadness will grow further apart as time goes on, but the loss itself will never go away.

Healing is not only a process of time. I could dwell in discomfort and sadness for years and never heal. Time alone is not the answer; it's the processing of emotions and acceptance that brings healing.

Society seems to want to push me onto some arbitrary timeline, demanding a clear separation between grief and okay-ness. But grief and okay-ness are not mutually exclusive. I do not simply "grieve" and then "move on." I process, and I carry forward. The anguish of loss will coexist with my okay-ness.

Forever.

Being a widower is not a stain on my life. It is not something to be pitied or feared, though it certainly feels that way sometimes, when I pay attention to the word choices and emotional weight people bring into conversations, pushing me further to the outside.

I expect I will fall in love again while still carrying the sadness of losing Ariana.

I will desire someone else while still carrying my love for her.

I have gained more than I have lost in life.

I refuse to waste what I have been given.

What hides beneath my surface?

How do I find my happy again? I am broken
into a pile of pieces. My systems don't function.
I feel nothing. How do I get back? How do I
move forward with my grief but let Ariana go?
　　　　　　　　　　- Apr 10, 2021 10:06 PM

BE BETTER

November 16, 2020

The turn signal ticked. I looked both ways, pulled out, and turned left. The song changed. It was our song. The soundtrack to *our* young love. I instinctively opened my mouth and started to sing along.

Not long after, my voice broke, my hands formed fists, and the sobbing began.

The core of life, for me, is to be deeply and completely known. That is what I had, and what I have lost. I feel like I'm in a universe of my own now, with no gravity to pull me into orbit around anyone.

The holidays are coming, and I've become absorbed with minimizing any changes to traditions, wanting life to feel, for the kids, as close as possible to how it was when Ariana was still here. And to that end, I feel I have to do it all myself.

I refuse to accept that I might be incapable of doing the work of two parents. The standards I set for myself won't allow me to give in or admit defeat. *I have to be better. I must be better.* I don't want anything to appear different to anyone looking in from the outside.

I want to be stronger, more adept, more capable than seems humanly possible.

I want to *be* okay, partly so I can eventually help others going through what I have.

I want to succeed, to cope, to parent, to an undeniable degree.

But underneath it all, I think I just want to never, ever, even for a moment, let Ariana down again. I want to somehow make up for all the times I was anything less than perfect for her.

Yet, I can't stop tripping over and stomping on my heart.

I retreat further into myself, trying to reel my heart back in. But then I become emotionally oversubscribed, stretched too thin, and disconnect from myself and my kids.

I fail over and over again.

So I continue to push because it's all I know how to do.

Until next week, when my therapist yells at me.

Again.

Sometimes all we can do is smile on the inside...

I'M SORRY, YOU DESERVE BETTER

January 20, 2021

I turned the water off, squeezed the sponge, and put it beside the sink. I turned to check the time: 10:56 PM. Pain shot down my neck. I had every intention, again, of being in bed by 10:00 PM, but my intentions feel meaningless nowadays.

From the moment I wake up, I run from responsibility to responsibility.

Work. Kids. House. People. I'm late for everything because I try to fit it all in. I feel like I can't catch my breath or find space to think, let alone breathe. My mental capacity feels diminished.

The haze of the holidays has started to wash away. The numbness required to get through them is fading. Restless, I turned the house upside down and removed everything from its place only to put it back again.

I am angry. Frustrated. Hurt. Physically and emotionally.

I feel like I am quickly becoming no good to anyone or anything.

My kids suffer from having an overworked and overstressed Dad. I feel I've lost all sense of kindness and patience with them. Sometimes, all I see are three humans who require more of me than I have left to give. I've forgotten how to have fun with them without somehow belittling them or yelling out of sheer stress. They lost their Mom, and now it feels as if they're losing their Dad too.

My phone fills with notifications I have every intention of addressing, but it's often midnight before I even glance at them. By then, I've run out of the mental energy required to read, respond, and care. So I tell myself, Tomorrow.

But tomorrow never happens.

I have no time for anyone. No time for myself.

I cannot love the way I want.

I cannot be the Dad I want to be.

The employee I strive to be.

The friend I used to be.

There are hurting men going through what I am who I want to lift up and support. There are people in my life I love so much, yet I cannot give my all to them. It is painful to look in the mirror and see this hopelessly lost man staring back.

I feel like I am good for nothing. And I feel it deep down; it's palpable. My life feels like it has lost meaning and purpose.

All day, every day, I push myself towards my breaking point, knowing I am only retreating deeper into myself and fearing that at some point, I won't be able to resurface.

It feels like there is no way out of this except through it.

Everyone in my life deserves better of me.

You deserve better of me.

I'm sorry.

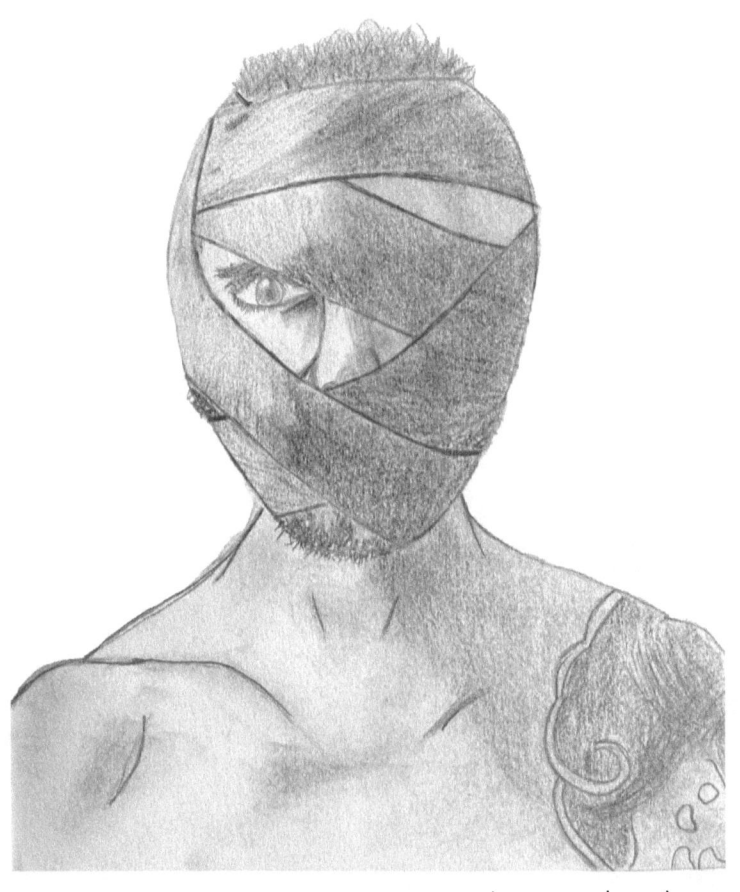

self-portrait
08.28.21

RECURSIVE

February 14, 2021

My chin rested on her head. I clenched my jaw, pulling her closer. My tears dropped into her dark brown hair. We embraced in silence; no words were uttered. The fan spun its tiny metal blades, whirling and humming, doing its best to pull the humidity from the bathroom. Our breath, hers and mine, moved slowly in and out, shallow, in rhythm with the fan. I could feel her heartbreak and wondered if she could feel mine.

Her cheer competition was approaching. It would be the first one since Ariana died. The first competition she wouldn't hear her mom cheering louder than the rest, the first Ariana wouldn't be there to get her ready. And it was the first one I had to handle solo. I felt in over my head, disconnected, desperately trying to show up for my daughter but feeling too broken and tired to truly be there.

I wiped my eyes and did my best to tell her I loved her, reassuring her that Mommy would still be there in spirit. I released my grip. We left the bathroom, and the morning continued.

I went down to my office and spent the afternoon trying to work while listening to the kids run back and forth overhead. Every so often, I would check in: make sure the house wasn't on fire, ensure they were in their Zoom classes, change a load of laundry, pick up a stray sock or piece of paper. And almost without fail, I would end up yelling at one of them.

The day wore on. The sun began to fade. Anxiety gradually filled my body, working its way up from my stomach into my lungs, suffocating me.

Work continued.

Later, I went upstairs with my laptop. I turned the oven dial to 350°F, threw four potatoes onto a tray, and put them in. Then I went back to my laptop for another meeting. It was getting late, too late for a proper dinner. The kids felt it; I felt it. Tension built, and the fighting began, each kid yelling at the other, distracting me. Finally, I picked up my laptop, moved back down to my office, and shut the door.

Work continued.

The potatoes were forgotten. Dried out, burned, inedible. The hours crept on and the kids were finally rescued by my parents: fed, put to bed. Their dad was nowhere in sight.

My heart shook. Ariana's death played over and over in my mind like a video on repeat: the progression, the final moments, the last time she spoke to me, the emptiness she left behind. Her absence filled my office. I stared blankly at the floating heads on my screen. I bit down hard on my tongue and squeezed my eyes shut. I reached for the mouse, disabled my video and audio, quickly double-checked they were off, and then collapsed to the floor.

My eyes flooded with tears. My throat ached. I bit down harder on my tongue, choking back screams. Eventually, it subsided. I wiped my face, took a deep breath, and got back up. Forcing a smile, I enabled my video and audio and got back to work.

When the work was completed, I said my goodbyes and put my computer to sleep. I checked my watch: 11:00 PM. I dug my knuckles into my eyes, massaging away the exhaustion. I left my office and went upstairs to the bedroom, walked to the bed, and sat down. I looked in the mirror opposite the bed. I felt pain, frustration, sadness, and anger course through my veins. I fell onto my side, grabbed my pillow, and screamed into it, crying until I couldn't anymore. I felt like I was back at

Ariana's bedside, crying over her body again, reliving the night my soul ripped from hers in those early morning hours.

This continued until I lost my voice and my eyes were dry. I pushed the pillow aside, got up, and walked to the bathroom. I washed my face, brushed my teeth, and made my way back to bed. I lay in silence for the next hour, trying to settle my body and soothe my mind, waiting for sleep to find me.

I felt lost again, overwhelmed by a sense of brokenness and failure. I wasn't the dad I wanted to be, not the dad I used to be. My mind taunted me with images of how I might have failed Ariana in life and how I felt I was failing her memory in death.

I closed my eyes only to find no rest, knowing I would have to do this all over again tomorrow. A cycle on repeat.

You see, I am not a single parent. I am a widower. It is different. Not worse. Not better. Just different.

There is a weight that sits permanently now, inches below my throat. Every day, it's there. The first thing I feel in the morning and the last thing I feel before bed. I have to carry it all day, holding it down until I inevitably can't anymore. It takes energy and stamina just to live with it, to care for it, to hold space for it. It takes constant effort and labor to balance this weight; too much tilt to one side, and it threatens to crush me.

I live happy and broken. Simultaneously.

Ariana is gone. Forever.

The kids lost their mother; I lost my best friend. We had no choice but to become motherless and a widower. We cannot change that. So we move forward within it.

We lose ourselves.

We lose each other.

But somehow, we keep finding our way back.

I am a broken man. A man with broken dreams, a broken body, and a broken heart.

For the first time in my life, I don't know how to pick up the pieces. Each day is a labored survival, soaked in tears.

I am not a single parent.

I'm a widower.

"... There is an unsettling in me, and uneasy that has compelled me to go room by room and tear it apart. Pull out everything from all hidden crevices and throw away anything useless and put back only those things that are necessary for survival.

A need to see everything that exist in the house and know it, feel it, and remember it. To figure out my own routines, my own reckoning with keeping the house afloat.

And in this chaos my kids are lost. The only parent they have now is their tablet. It entertains them. Teaches them. Shows them love. A mechanical cold love in the absence of their father. Who has no words but frustration and disappointment for every little thing they do wrong. Every time they get in the way. Every time I misunderstand because I'm too busy in my own world..."

— Jan 20, 2021 6:16 PM

THIRTY-SIX

March 10, 2021

Surprise breakfast in bed from my kids, complete with food weighed out. It was both amazingly sweet and heartbreaking.

There is much to celebrate today: my birthday, the amazing work of my peers on a historic day for my employer, and Ariana's "cancerversary." This would have marked the sixth year of her life with cancer.

Ariana was supposed to be here, celebrating all these moments and milestones with me. Instead, I'm here watching my kids spend more time caring for me, worrying about their Dad, than taking care of themselves.

The weight my kids carry is more than they should ever have to shoulder. The amount of worry and sadness they hold, watching their Dad struggle with grief, is profoundly unfair.

This breakfast represents the amazing team I have in my kids. It's also a painful reminder that I feel unable to be the Dad I want to be.

I feel I am, and perhaps will continue to be, a broken man with a dysfunctional mind, body, and spirit.

So today, I honor Ariana by dipping into her scotch. I partake, letting the warmth and burn of the drink fill my body. I let it remind me of my best friend. Remind me of the pain my kids experience every day. Remind me of the lessons Ariana taught me. Remind me that I once had it all.

I miss you, Ariana.

The kids miss you.

And it is tearing me apart.

THE PATH

March 11, 2021

I ran upstairs to the bedroom. My right foot stepped into the room first. I stopped, turned, and looked in the mirror. My head tilted. I paused. I had completely forgotten why I was there.

My shoulders shrugged. I walked out of the room, made my way downstairs stepping over the boys glued to their iPads, then into the living room and onto the couch.

I let my head hang back, focusing on the ceiling. My eyes swelled; I felt flushed with sadness. I closed my eyes and waited for her voice. Only silence came. Then tears. Then anger.

I searched my body and mind for anything worth fighting for now. I had fought for a future with Ariana, then for the present with her. I had purpose. I had a plan. I had a life. I had... well, I felt I'd had it all.

But there, on that couch, with my head held back, I came up short.

I laid my hands on my face; they felt foreign. *The kids need me. Get up. Get up!* I argued silently with the person whose body I felt I was only renting.

My legs started to move. My arms pushed into the couch, bringing me to my feet. I looked around at what felt like a plastic world: lifeless, hollow.

This path I now walk feels filled with shards of glass. Each step is labored, painful. So, I retreat into myself out of survival, narrowing my focus to each single step. I place one foot carefully in front of the other, trying not to tread too hard, lest the glass pierce completely through my foot.

Every so often, someone comes along who offers me a seat, a moment of rest. I smile, say thank you, and sit for a while, though I'm still writhing internally as the glass remains embedded in my feet. As the moments pass, I realize it's best to get back up and keep moving forward.

I look towards those ahead of me who still walk this path. Their feet are scarred, calloused; the glass shards seem to have taken up permanent residence there. Their eyes, however, are not always fixated on each step. Yet every so often, a shard hits just right, and pain shoots through their body–a reminder they are still on the path.

I will never get to leave this path. I will walk, always, with glass beneath my feet. My kids will walk, always, with glass beneath their feet.

So standing there in the living room, I tried to remember her laugh, to conjure her smile, to hear her tell me it's okay. I tried to remember what it felt like to live life fully despite suffering, to remember her lessons.

And in that moment, I realized I had forgotten how to smile while suffering, or perhaps I never really knew how.

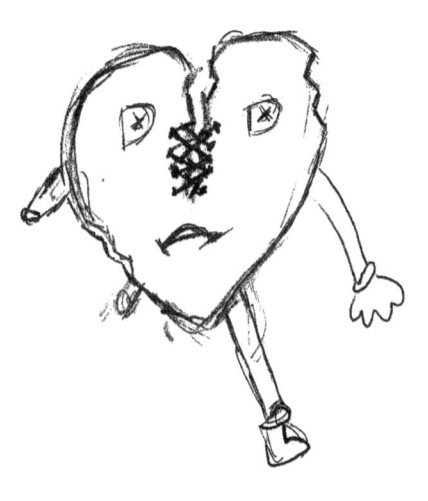

Art has always been a therapy for me.
Creating, expressing, letting everything
go onto my canvas of choice.

THE SWEETNESS

March 25, 2021

And sometimes, the weight of grief crushes you.

It presses down on your shoulders, compressing your spine until your ribs feel like they might crack. Your lungs shorten, threatening to collapse; breathing becomes difficult. Your heart feels pinched between your ribs with a force strong enough to shear it. Your stomach grows queasy. Your knees buckle. Your ankles pop. You crash to the floor.

Your body is laid out, shaking.

It's an all-out existential crisis. Your systems feel like they are no longer functioning. Your mind seems to push out from your body, and then the thoughts hit: *Why her? Why not me? Who decided I was uniquely qualified to handle this? She had so much more to give this world than I ever will. So why am I the one left behind?* You panic. You worry. You fear everything, true and untrue. You convince yourself you are too weak to have endured what she did, that you could never laugh, smile, and enjoy life with death staring you in the face.

You scream internally, *"Move, body! Fucking move!"*

It takes a second, but somehow it works. Your body starts listening. You slowly come back into your shell, yet it takes everything you have just to perform the basics. What used to be automatic now requires concentrated, concerted effort. It's as if you're doing everything for the first time again.

All sweetness in life has turned sour.

Your tongue feels numb from sampling everything in your path, desperate to taste sweetness one more time. You want to laugh again, to really smile again, but you realize so much of that was her. She was the center. You flew in her orbit; now that she is gone, you wander aimlessly, spinning out of control. You cannot find your own gravity. Everything feels bland and pointless without her to share it with.

And for the first time, you are older than her.

Life moves on, whether you want it to or not. Her voice grows fainter. Her smell, her laugh, her very spirit feel more distant. Each day, you carry it forward, both your grief and yourself, this new, overtly flawed human you have become. Your facial features remain the same, but everything inside has changed. Part of you died when she died. Yet everyone seems to want the old you back. They want you "better," "fixed," "okay," mainly so they can feel okay.

So you turn yourself upside down to smile.

A BRIEF
INTERMISSION:
LIFE UPDATES

I have forgotten how to smile and
suffer, or, maybe, I never even know how.
Plastic emotions.
Changed human.
— Mar 6, 2021 1:14 PM

04.02.2021

For the past three weeks, Charlie has been passed between doctors as they tried to determine what was growing in his neck. For three weeks, I've had to walk the same agonizing steps with Charlie that I first walked with Ariana six years ago.

And again, I found myself sitting in a doctor's office, hearing words like "hard mass" and "cancer" thrown around loosely. I never imagined this would happen again; certainly not so soon, and not involving my son. But there we sat while three doctors drilled Charlie with questions, mostly staring at the floor, giving us no real answers. It was hell. Pure hell. At the end of the appointment, they concluded the only way forward was to remove the mass and test it for cancer.

I took a deep breath, helped Charlie from his chair, and walked to the front desk to schedule his surgery. We got the information, walked back to the car, and headed home. The car was silent until Charlie finally spoke: "Do I have cancer?" I didn't know how to answer him. I wanted to say, *No, buddy, there's no way,* but I couldn't lie to him.

So we moved through the next week, day by day, until the surgery. Charlie did his best to live normally, despite the waves of panic that clearly moved through him, filling our home. He reminded me so much of Ariana in that way, doing his best to smile through the fear.

Wednesday came, and he made it through surgery. The surgeon took nearly double the expected time to remove the mass. "It was a lot bigger than we anticipated," he mentioned afterwards.

Today, while playing with Charlie, my phone rang. It was

the doctor. I picked it up and was immediately bombarded with questions: "How is he doing?" "Is he having trouble swallowing?" "Can he move his tongue?" My mind raced. *Why the fuck is he asking me all these questions?* My reply to each was simply, "He seems okay." Only then did the doctor tell me that the mass they pulled from Charlie's neck was a type of nerve tumor documented in only four other medical reports, ever. Charlie was one of maybe five people known to have had this type of tumor. It was only after dropping that piece of information that the doctor finally told me the tumor was 100 percent benign. We would need to follow up in six months for an MRI, but otherwise, Charlie was okay.

It's hard to explain what this experience was like for me. It is difficult to convey the feeling of reliving the horror from six years ago, particularly having to do it alone this time. What *is* clear, though, is that there is an excessive amount of lingering trauma in my system that needs to be worked through and released.

The world has felt unsafe for so long; this experience only further entrenched that belief.

My kids have been through enough. I just want them to have a break.

To be kids.

To not have to worry about this shit.

Maybe I deserve this life, but they don't.

"I wanted to bring awareness to grief and mental health support, so I started my efforts to launch a clothing brand, **'Hopeless Mope'**, where you can wear your feelings..."

04.22.2021

I get tons of joy and excitement from cooking for people. As Massimo Bottura says, "Cooking is an act of love." That is truer now than ever for me. But I don't like to make a habit of cooking something for the first time when serving others.

Better to practice before serving.

It's hard to relate to people post-widowhood. My view of the world has changed; I have changed. My openness comes and goes. I seem to have little control over whom I might connect with, or when the floodgates might unexpectedly open.

There is a strong tendency to isolate. I often begin the day already emotionally taxed by the simplest things, like just getting out of bed. This leaves little room for much else.

Think about how exhausted you feel after a good crying session. It's like that, only multiplied by a very large number, every single day.

So I turn to my writing and cooking. It is how I can remain open without *having* to be open socially.

It keeps me close to those I've lost. I keep pushing myself, hoping that someday someone might say, "He bakes like Ariana and cooks like his Dad." Her desserts and his food represented something far beyond the physical sensation of eating.

A story, or stories, for another day.

"There is no warning when the grief hits. Or why it hits. Or how hard it will hit. You could go days or weeks with little episodes here and there only to be decimated with one big blow.

The only thing you can do is let it come, let it run its course and hope you are alone.

Today, after it all came out, I found myself left with a sense of hopelessness. Which is not uncommon, but it came after a week of feeling so much hope. A week of feeling a sense of purpose. A week of feeling clarity and direction."

EXPRESS FEARLESSLY

*The many iterations of Hopeless Mope.

[123]

05.09.2021

I have had no mental or physical energy for workouts since Ariana died. They just aren't the same.

Not even close. I have no sense of a future self.

So it makes inducing short-term pain for long-term results feel almost impossible.

But I keep doing it anyway, going through the motions, keeping my body moving.

There are many things in my life right now that my mind cannot engage with, but thankfully my body seems to be moving on muscle memory, just waiting for my mind to eventually catch up.

05.30.2021

Cognitive dysfunction. That's something I am struggling badly to accept as part of my grief journey. Certainly, it's better than it was in the beginning, but I still don't feel like myself.

I am frustrated every day: frustrated that I cannot remember things, frustrated that normal, mundane tasks require enormous amounts of energy I just don't have.

I wake up each day hoping it will be different, hoping I will suddenly snap back to my old self, but that's never the case.

So I continually search for tiny improvements, little glimpses suggesting I'm getting better. Really, anything to hold on to.

This whole experience makes you desperate for time just to sit, with no expectations placed upon you. Time when no one needs you, when there are no emails to answer, no dates to schedule for the thousands of things the kids require.

But when you actually carve out that time, the guilt piles on. You feel guilty for not taking care of the endless list of tasks, for not spending all your free time with the kids, for not responding to that text your friend sent two days ago.

It's an endless cycle of exhaustion, guilt, and desperation, compounded by the things you continuously see yourself failing at.

So instead of resting, you push and push until you literally wake up after passing out on the floor while folding laundry.

Again.

And so I try to convince myself I'll be better tomorrow.

"I drew 'slow down' sloth to remind myself it's
OK to slow down in the midst of everything
crashing into you.
Or maybe I was asking the world to slow down
for a minute.. ?"

09.22.2021

I'm not okay. I haven't admitted that enough this year. So, I'm saying it now.

I lost my person of 17 years. All I wanted was to grow old with Ariana.

I lost my world in a single instant. One moment, I had her; the next, I didn't.

I can't explain what this feels like and, honestly, I'm tired of trying. It's inexplicable. It's constant. It's never-ending.

I'm not okay.

And today, I crashed hard into that reality. I couldn't stop crying. It didn't matter where I was: in a work meeting, in line at Wegmans, sitting in my room alone drawing. The tears just came. The sobbing came. Eventually, I had to just let go and not care that people could see me.

My private habit became public.

As the anniversary of her death creeps closer, my mental state grows heavier. It feels like I'm reliving the hell all over again, the physical and emotional pain returning.

I don't want to relive it. I already lived through it once. I don't want to do it again. But I seem to have little choice in the matter.

So, I carry on.

Because I'm not okay.

And why the fuck would I be okay? I spent years with death staring me in the face, thinking about disease and dying as if it were normal. Those experiences are firmly planted in my subconscious; they have wrecked me.

So, no, I'm not okay. But I will persevere.

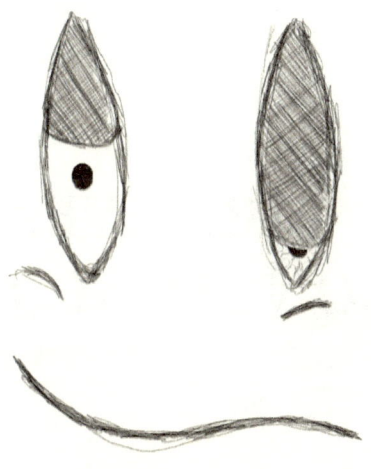

THE FIRST YEAR:
CONTINUED

Mr. Anxiety

his tentacles get
everywhere

THE ANNIVERSARY

July 14, 2021

To My Ariana,

It's our first anniversary apart, and I wish I could tell you that I was okay, but that lie is hard to keep up. I've tried, I really have. I had myself convinced for a short while, but I still haven't figured out how to sleep without you. And I'm so tired. So incredibly tired.

I love you. I just need you to know that.

I've changed since the day you left me. You took half of my heart, and I haven't been the same. The world is lonely, scary, and painful. I'm not the man you married. I'm confused all the time. Exhausted. Stressed. I'm late for everything. I forget everything. I drown myself in distractions.

I've lost my spark.

And I'm scared you wouldn't love the man I've become. I've lost my way. I lost you, my true north.

The kids and I have drifted into our own worlds of suffering. Each one of us deals with it in our own ways. We aren't a family anymore. My arms aren't strong enough to hold us together.

I can't keep up, babe. School, work, sports, laundry, cooking, cleaning, kids, dogs, plants, email... all of it. I can't do it. The kids need me, they need me so badly, and I'm just not there. I am so sorry I am failing our children in their pain.

Also, would you believe me if I told you the kids had enough of eating rice and chicken? I don't blame them.

Their birthdays and holidays aren't the same without you. I can't live up to your standard. And I see the look of disappointment on the kids' faces.

Oh, I forgot, Charlie had a tumor in his neck, can you

believe that? Back in March. We had a month of testing that ended in surgery to remove it. It felt like I was with you all over again. I had to tell our son he might have cancer. It was so scary. I needed you then. I needed your strength and assurance. Thankfully, it ended okay. It was benign. I only wish you had the same outcome.

Being around anyone is hard now, too. I am constantly looking over my shoulder, half expecting to see you there at family and social gatherings. It's exhausting, on top of already being exhausted. I do what I can, but it's not enough. Everyone just thinks I am anti-social for the sake of being anti-social.

I forget to text people back all the time. Sometimes I don't have enough energy to respond. It's hard to explain. Trying to explain it also requires energy. So, it's easier to let people think what they want about me than to explain how emotionally taxing social interaction is, or that I'm in a constant state of holding back tears.

The good news is that I've stopped crying in front of people. I'm sure they've had enough. So my grief is a "me" thing now. I've been practicing my smile and "I'm okay," though I'm sure it's not fooling anyone. I still wait until I'm alone to let it all go. It usually breaks through at my desk, in the car, or in the shower. The best is when the house is quiet, and no one is around. That's when I can really dig in, screaming and crying.

I miss you, Ariana. I don't think I can stress that enough.

Every day I obsess over my shortcomings and things I could have done better.

I'm sorry I didn't tell you how much you meant to me more often.

I'm sorry for not being stronger for you, for not holding

you closer in your pain.

I'm sorry for letting work take so much of my stress and mental energy.

I'm sorry you had to protect me from your pain.

I'm sorry for hurting you in any way.

You were truly the best part of us, and the more I am without you, the more I see that. All that is good in me is because you taught me and pushed me to be better.

I'm so scared those good things are being stripped away by my grief. As time goes on, I will fall more and more into the broken pieces I was before I met you.

I am struggling with work.

I am struggling to be a dad.

I am struggling to be a brother, son, nephew, and friend.

The pain I am carrying is enormous and intense.

My dreams haunt me.

I feel sick all the time.

I feel guilty all the time.

Your memory hurts me.

But I keep reminding myself that the sickness and pain I carry are nothing compared to what you held.

You amazed me, and I will hold onto your strength. I will remember you. I will always be grateful you chose to spend your life with me, even if I still struggle to believe you could have loved me.

I think about you every day. I worry whether you are okay. I fear that you can see my loneliness and pain, and I worry that it causes you to suffer at my expense.

If it's possible, please let me know if you are okay. And please, I beg you to look away from me and only remember our good times. Remember who I was with you, not what I've become.

Marrying you was the best decision of my life. I'll never forget the party you designed and planned for us 14 years ago.

Thank you for choosing me and giving me a chance to grow.

With love,
Your husband.

I AM | RAISED BY |
AM | WOMEN |

WHO I AM

BECAUSE OF

WOMEN

THE AVOCADO

August 10, 2021

I flipped the light switch off and walked out of the bathroom into my room. I paused and looked down at a shirt left on the floor. I slid my foot under the shirt, kicked upwards, and caught it midair with my right hand. Then I threw it into the dirty pile of clothes.

"Two minutes, I'm coming to tuck everyone in. Your shit better be picked up. All your clothes, blankets, and stuffed animals better be in your rooms and put away," I yelled. I walked towards my bed and grabbed my pajamas, unfolded them, and put them on, exchanging my jeans for sweatpants. I folded my jeans, went to the closet, and put them away.

Afterward, I walked out of my closet and headed toward the door. I stopped. My breathing shallowed. My fists balled. I clenched my teeth. I took two steps and grabbed my son's Avocado stuffed animal, aptly named Avoie, sitting on the floor in the doorway of my room.

I squeezed it tightly. All the contents in my stomach rushed up to my throat. I opened my mouth to yell. Nothing came out. *How many times do I need to tell him to pick up his shit? How many times?*

I squeezed Avoie tighter and looked into its green dotted eyes. I scowled at it, and it only smiled back. I released my grip, exposing its dark brown pit for a belly. I remembered my son getting Avoie for Christmas last year. It was our first Christmas without Ariana, and all he wanted was this stuffed Avocado. He held stuffed animals in high regard. To him, they possessed magical power. They could make you feel less scared, less nervous, and less sad when held. They were the protectors of his world. But Avoie... well, he held Avoie higher than the rest.

I looked away from Avoie and into the big picture window

next to me in the hallway. All the bile that had rushed to my throat dropped to my stomach. My hand shook. My mouth quivered.

What am I doing? Why am I so angry all the time?

Avoie had been carefully placed at my door. Its body was facing in, staring into my room, watching over me. My son had not forgotten to pick up his stuffed animal out of willful ignorance. No, he was trying to help me. It was his final attempt to connect. He hasn't been reaching for my hand every day because he needs something from me; he just wanted to hold me. He left Avoie so that its magic might comfort his Daddy and make him feel okay.

I wrinkled my face to hold back the tears, turned around, walked back to my bed, and carefully placed the stuffed Avocado between my pillows.

I walked to each of the kids' rooms, tucked them in, kissed them, said goodnight, and shut their doors. I turned off the lights in the hallway and headed toward my bed. I pulled the comforter and sheets down, crawled into bed, grabbed Avoie, and held it tightly in my arms while it soaked up my tears. I embraced its magic and fell asleep.

ONE YEAR; FOREVER CHANGED

october 10, 2021

My back became sore, lying against the wooden floor. I shifted my legs and swept my arms up and down. My body danced around, searching for a comfortable position so I could get a few hours of sleep. Above me on the bed, the kids were laid out like puzzle pieces. Each one was careful not to kick or roll into her. She was finally resting, sleeping, existing halfway between this world and the next. It was her first night of hospice.

I stared at the ceiling. There was nothing left for me to do but try to sleep and prepare myself for the days ahead. I closed my eyes, and everything began to darken. My vision faded into something like a dream. I dropped into a void of nothingness. My body was paralyzed.

I felt myself looking through her eyes and sensed her floating between two worlds. I began to shake. I lost control of my body, overwhelmed by the experience. Then a voice emerged. A faint whisper. "CJ... CJ... C," it repeated. Ariana called out to me. My body bent in half. I gasped for air. Stood up and ran to her side.

"Hey, babe. I'm here. What is it? What do you need?," I asked, my body still shaking.

"CJ. It's time."

"It's time for what?" I asked.

"I'm ready. I'm ready to go. It's time. Call everyone," Ariana whispered.

My stomach shifted. I moved away from the bed and reached for my phone. I stood up and began pacing the floor of our room. I made my way down the list of family. One by one, waking them up, and insisting they come back. Every few steps, I looked over at the bed. The kids and Ariana were saying their goodbyes.

"I love you," Ariana told them.

"No. No... mommy," the kids cried.

"It's okay. It's time for me to go. I love you guys so much."

"Mommy... no... mommy."

My hands became uncontrollable. Shaking. Trembling. My family started to show up. They all took their turn, saying their goodbyes. I watched from a distance. I stayed focused on everyone else. It was too much for my mind to accept what was happening. But the night wore on. My throat burned, and my head throbbed. And soon, I found myself in bed.

I looked over at her, and I broke. I crawled over her unmoving body. I closed my eyes and felt a hand reaching into my chest. It searched around, looking for my heart, grabbed hold, and squeezed as hard as it could. I screamed, breaking my silence. My body convulsed, and I underwent a pain I had never felt before. I cried. My tears poured over Ariana, and the pain grew. Then the hand released its grip. I took a breath and felt it rooting again, searching for my soul. It pulled on the edges, tearing at the seams. Ripping my soul from hers. It was a surgery of the most barbaric kind. I wept. I screamed. I writhed in pain.

The night crept, and dawn teased its light. Slowly, each person found their spot in the house, and when their tears ran dry, they fell asleep.

And for the next five days, the house was filled with food, people, laughter, and pain. Each day Ariana grew more distant. "She" disappeared. She retreated into an unknown world while her body did its best to fight a losing battle.

On one of those days, desperate to feel her spirit again,

I lay next to her on the bed. I moved my hand towards hers, slowly and carefully holding it in mine. I turned to her and whispered in her ear.

"Ariana, if you can hear me, I need you to know how much I love you and how much I will miss you. I am so grateful for everything you did for me, gave me, and taught me. I will never forget you. I will never stop loving you."

Her legs shot up, and her eyes popped open. I smiled and squeezed her hand tighter. I looked into her eyes and only saw pain. I panicked. She started to move erratically, so I jumped out of bed. My sister and uncle ran to her side to help her. I walked out of the room and out of that reality.

I paced the hallway and repeatedly whispered, *"I hurt her. I hurt her. I'm failing to let her die in peace."* My sight dimmed, and all the times I failed her played in a loop before my eyes. Fists formed, and I began to beat my sides. My spirit was pulled from my body. It was unable to bear the failure. And at that moment, the only person who could bring me back was dying in my bed.

Ariana settled again. Calm. Drugged. My uncle walked out of the room and towards me. He grabbed my arms to calm my beating. "You didn't do anything wrong, CJ." He repeated until my spirit rested back in my body. But the seed of hatred for myself was firmly planted that day.

I walked back into the room and to her bedside. I dropped to the floor, too afraid to be near her. Too scared to hurt her again.

A few more days passed until the morning of September 30, 2020. Her breathing was slow and shallow. We were tired. We needed it to end. For her to be at peace. She wasn't there anymore. So we decided to make it quiet for her. Hoping she needed stillness to move on. I opened the window. The cool breeze blew over her head. *She is beautiful, even in her death.* I kissed her head and walked out of the room. To leave her to be alone.

I went downstairs to the kitchen table. I pulled the chair out and sat down. Conversations became background noise. My thoughts were consumed with death. *Is she alive? Will I walk in, and she'll be gone?* I looked around. Everyone was too tired to hide their pain. Their faces bent, they casually sat around a table waiting for and giving space to someone so they could die.

Time carried on. I stood up from the table and walked upstairs to the bedroom door. I paused. My hand reached for the handle. Trembled. I turned the knob, closed my eyes, and slid into the room.

I didn't know what I wanted to see when I opened my eyes. *How would I feel if she was dead? What would I do if she was still breathing? Was I strong enough to lose her, even though she was already gone?*

I opened my eyes and watched her chest. Nothing. Nothing. Nothing. Movement. My shoulders dropped. My Sun, Stars, Moon, and World lay bare, like an animal trapped in its own mind, reduced to her family watching her, waiting for her final breath.

I walked to the chair by her bedside and collapsed into it, rested my chin in my hands, and began talking. "Ariana. My love. I will be okay. You have prepared me. You have shown me and taught me all that I need to know. You have left me with more than I ever could have asked for. Thank you for everything you did for me, for our kids. So many people have come to our aid, and I now see that they care about me. That it isn't just you that they cared about. I'm sorry I couldn't see that before, but now I see. It's okay, my sweet. Please go be at peace. No more pain. Please free yourself from your pain. You fought hard enough. I'm so proud of you."

I leaned back in the chair. My back ached. My head pounded. It was not unlike the years I'd spent at her side in hospitals and doctors' offices, including the nights and early mornings sleeping upright in hospital waiting rooms. I had spent the past five years waiting. Waiting for more bad news. Waiting for more pain. But mostly waiting to run to her and help her. And now, that was done. There was nothing left for me to do for her. I felt lost. Scared and so alone.

I suffered. Ariana suffered more.

The rest of the family joined me. We all sat quietly by her. Watching her. The seconds grew between each breath. One more breath. Then her jaw tightened. Released. Over.

I fell back onto the floor. My son crumpled and screamed. I watched as his entire world fell before him. I realized then that I was alone to care for them. And I worried. How would I get them through this? Everyone left the room. The kids and I stayed behind. We said our final goodbye and walked out.

I spent the next year learning how to live without her. Learning how to be "CJ" and not "CJ & Ariana." I watched as my family of four split apart. Grieving alone. Only to begin to find our way back to each other.

I ripped the house apart and put it back together. I failed and succeeded and then failed again. I forgot conversations I had with people. I missed appointments. I was never on time. I didn't sleep. I cried. I screamed. I laughed. I screamed, and then I cried.

I was angry, sad, broken, lost, and numb. I yelled at Ariana. I talked to her nearly every day, begging her to come back. I asked her to protect our son during his surgery to remove his tumor. But, most of all, I apologized for all my failures and prayed for her to forgive me.

I lived my life still trying to please her. I spent my days worrying about her. Hoping to find some way I could protect her and make her feel loved.

I am now in charge of her legacy. The stories I tell about her. The way I speak about her. The light I shed on our moments together. There is no fact-checker, and my mind bends and breaks at the thought of misrepresenting her. She is worthy of the truth. She is worthy of the legacy she built and how she cared for me, the kids, and those who came into her life. She is owed everything.

And now, with a year of life over without her, I carry on. As I reflect on the past 17 years of having Ariana by my side, I note everything she gave to me. I see all the ways she loved me. The ways she lived so selflessly for the kids and me. I see all she did to support me in whatever endeavor I set out to do. She believed in me with her whole heart. And I know, I would not be where I am today without her by my side. I would not be the person I am, the father I am, or the friend I am, without her.

And after a year, I still reluctantly go to bed each night and find myself drowning in a deep well of nothingness. No matter how much I laugh or cry, no matter what is different about the day, they all end the same. I have learned that this nothingness will remain. It will never leave me. It is only my capacity to carry it that grows.

To you, who have held me up this past year when I could not carry myself, I will always have deep gratitude for you. To those who have been patient and honest with me, sat and listened to me, thank you. You, who, of all the things you could do, chose to read my ramblings, my heart is full because of you. And to my brothers who are walking the path I have walked, I will always be here for you.

My love to you all.

EPILOGUE

THE RETREAT

I sat, staring out the window. The sun was stinging my
eyes, which were dry from the long flight. Three other men
continued their talking—surface talk, the kind you make when
you first meet someone, when they are still a stranger. My
mouth remained closed. I did my best to let the sound of the
conversation fade into the background. My mind stuck on one
thought: *"Why the hell did I sign up to come out here, and why
did I agree to hitch a ride with some other men from the airport?
This is my nightmare."*

After about an hour, we pulled into the driveway that led
to a towering structure: a large barn converted into a retreat
space, tucked away in the Texas landscape. The tires crunched
over the gravel until we came to a stop. I got out of the car,
grabbed my luggage, and braced for whatever was about to
come. As I walked down the makeshift sidewalk to the door, I
was greeted by smiling faces and warm welcomes.

Inside, it felt smaller and colder. It was an open space that
would challenge everything I thought I knew about grief and
vulnerability. It was the place that would become a turning
point in my grief journey.

Stalls ran along the walkway, which was dotted with
a smattering of old, worn carpets and random furniture—
couches and chairs—forming mini-sections for conversation.
At the end of the walkway was a single bathroom with
four shower stalls and sinks. It was a minimalist and rustic

environment that felt both imposing and intimate. Each of us had a bed in a stall, creating a sense of separation but ultimately fostering unexpected community.

"Grab any open stall and get situated. We'll begin in an hour," I heard a voice call out behind me.

I stepped slowly down the walkway, peeking into each stall as I came upon it. About halfway down I found an empty one. I walked in, pushed the large sliding barn door shut and collapsed on the bed. *"I don't want to be here,"* I repeated to myself over and over until my eyes finally closed and I fell asleep.

I woke up to the sound of chairs sliding across the floor. I stood up on the bed and looked around my prison cell. I grabbed a mint from my backpack, walked over to the door and slid it open. In front of my door were cold, metal chairs, about twenty arranged in a large circle. At the top of the circle sat a small blue couch with the two leaders waiting for everyone to be seated. I took the seat immediately outside my door and sat down.

The leaders began by establishing the rules, explaining the weekend's structure. The longer they talked, the deeper I sank into my thoughts. I leaned over, put my head in my hands, and stared at the intricate patterns of red and gold in the carpet.

"Everyone clear on the rules?" said the leader.

"Yes," replied the men in the circle.

"Okay, let's go around now, and each person tell us why they are here and what you are hoping to get out of this weekend."

The introductions began on the other side of the circle. I listened with a mixture of anger and numbness, never lifting my gaze from the floor. Suddenly, the side door opened, and the setting sun poured into the barn. A man hurried in and sat down on the last open chair. He apologized for being late. I immediately felt a pull towards him. *"I need to speak with him. Something about him."* A few hours passed, and it was soon my turn to share why I was there. While others had spoken at length, I spoke for barely thirty seconds: "I'm here. I'm in grief. That's it." I felt the tears build up in my throat. *"Please don't ask me any follow-up questions."*

"Tell me about your grief," one of the leaders called out.

"Fuck." "Uh, well," my voice cracked as the tears breached my eyes, "my wife passed away last year. I have—uh—three kids. So—yeah. I'm here for that. I need a change," I said.

They offered a kind welcome and moved on to the next man sitting to my left. Another two hours passed, and we finally finished up for the night. My back ached from sitting on the plane all day and then in the hard metal chair for four hours. I went back to my room, slipped under the covers and fell asleep.

The lights in the barn flicked on. I blinked my eyes open, and after a few moments realized where I was. *"OK. Three more days."* Breakfast was being served and others were crowding the bathrooms trying to shower and get ready for the day. I ate breakfast first, hoping the bathroom would clear out by the time I finished. I sat alone, purposefully avoiding others. One by one, each man ate their food, washed up and found a seat back in the circle.

After the morning welcome, the leaders asked that we all stand up. We were then instructed to walk around the room, and every time we made eye contact with another man, we had to stop and hold eye contact. Ten seconds at first, then a minute, then two minutes.

After maybe 15 minutes of doing this—which felt like two hours—we were told to stop and partner up with the closest man standing in front of us and stare into each other's eyes, without breaking contact. I found myself standing in front of a towering man, the very same man who had walked in late on the first day. I looked at him and still felt the same stirring in my heart that I had felt the day before. As we maintained eye contact, the discomfort was overwhelming. Staring at a stranger, witnessing and being witnessed, swaying back and forth in a strange, almost dance-like movement.

Then came an instruction that would break something open inside me. We had to extend our arms and place our hands, one person with palms facing up, the other with palms facing down. My hands ended up on the top, hovering over this stranger's hands. Swaying continued. Discomfort continued. Then the leader's voice cut through the tension: "The person whose hands are on top, drop your hands and let the other man support you."

I let my hands fall until my fingertips touched my partner's hands. After a minute, one of the leaders walked by and noticed our hands. He looked directly at me. "CJ, drop your hands and let him hold you. Let him support you."

I paused. I took a breath and then reluctantly dropped my hands maybe another quarter of an inch, fully down into his hands. The moment my hands dropped, I began to shake. Tears flooded my eyes and I completely broke down. Both leaders were now at my side.

"Let yourself fall into your partner, CJ."

I shook my head 'no', yet my body disobeyed. I collapsed into this stranger's arms. My face pressed into his chest as I soaked his shirt in my tears. The other men began to surround me. I felt helpless against what was happening, against what was emerging.

The leaders encouraged me. "Scream. Let us hear what your pain sounds like." And I did: The most guttural, primal scream emerged from the depths of my being.

"If your pain had a voice, what would it say?" One leader asked.

"Support," I cried. "I haven't had support. I feel alone. I am so alone."

"Then let yourself be supported now."

My eyes remained closed and my head still firmly pressed against this man's chest. My face was pointed to the floor. I was held captive in my head–with blackness overtaking me. "CJ, are you okay if the men lift you up and hold you?" The leader asked. I nodded, and one by one, the men came around me. They lifted me, their arms and hands grasping each other below me. They built a hammock made of arms as I lay down with my face towards the ceiling. Every couple of minutes, I would feel one man's arms release their hold, and another man came in to take his place. They continued to hold me in the air, squeezing, creating a human cocoon of support. The leaders asked me to speak to Ariana. "What would she think about you right now? What would she feel? What would she want to tell you?"

The more I spoke to her and the more I answered their questions, the deeper my sobs became. What emerged from me released a knot of terror deep within my heart. The leader placed his hand flat onto my chest, "Breathe, CJ, breathe."

I felt my heart begin to slow and the muscles around my jaw, neck, and back began to loosen. Another minute of breathing, the muscles in my body relaxed into the arms of the men. I opened my eyes and looked around. I saw tears, constricted faces, and expressions not of pity, but of love, of witness.

They slowly brought my feet to the floor, and then lifted my back. My feet were planted on the floor, but my body swayed until the blood settled in all the places it belonged. I stood, speechless, and one by one each man came and hugged me.

We finished the day and after dinner, as the sun began to set, a fire was lit in the backyard. One by one, each of us found our way to the plastic, faux Adirondack chairs. I was late, walking to the group of men sharing stories, with the man whose shirt was still stained with my tears. We found our seats in the back, on the outskirts of the fire.

Chatter continued for the next hour as I began to share more of myself with my new friend. As the temperature dropped and the night wore on, we all agreed it was lights out. There was another full day ahead. I trekked back to the barn after the crowd had dissipated, stopped in my room to get my things, and quietly walked to the bathroom. After washing up, I tiptoed back to my stall, making sure not to wake anyone. I crawled into bed and slipped the thin, worn blanket over me, closed my eyes, and fell asleep with a smile in my heart.

The next morning continued just the same, with exercises meant to get us connected, pushing us in and out of our comfort zone. One by one, men were called into "the circle" as it became known. This was the call to dig deeper into what was happening inside and coming up for them. It was not voluntary, but requested by the leaders.

When you heard your name called to enter, you knew you were in for a painful, yet cathartic experience. You were not only entering into the center of the circle of men, but into the heart of your shadow. Not every man was called. And no one was asked to be in the circle more than once, that is, until I heard my name called.

Sitting on the opposite side from where my stall was this time, I found myself on the cold concrete floor. My back still aching, but I needed a break from the chairs. We had just come back from a fifteen-minute break where we were asked to journal and answer one of the questions posed to us. Then, as we did on the first day, we went around to each man as they shared what they wrote.

Because I was on the other side, my turn came up quickly. With less hatred, and diffused anger, I spoke aloud what I had written. The details are not as important as the events that followed. One of the leaders began to dig in and ask follow-up questions until, after one line of questioning, he struck the core of the emotion that I was struggling with. And I heard those words, again, "CJ, would you be open to coming into the circle?" I paused, looked around the room, and decided, reluctantly, to stand up and accept the invitation.

Seated on the floor, the leader came down to sit with me. His eyes met mine.

"CJ, I want you to close your eyes," he said. I complied.

"I'm going to come close to you and place my hand on

your back and your chest, is this okay?"

I nodded.

He moved swiftly to my side and I felt the warmth of his hands as he placed them with precision and care. It was a stark contrast to the cold I felt all over my body. "I want you to imagine Ariana is sitting in front of you," he requested. *Not this again.* I squeezed my eyes tighter and began to bring up the image of her sitting, legs crossed, staring at me. She began to smile, and the energy in the room fell to the background of my conscious awareness. All I could feel was Ariana, and all I could hear was the leader's voice.

"What is she saying to you?"

I shook my head, biting my bottom lip to hold back the emotions.

"CJ, what is she saying?"

"Uh–she is telling me that she loves me." The tears broke through.

"What do you want to say to her?"

"I…I love you and I miss you so much, but–I'm glad you're not in pain anymore, but I am so scared. I am so scared of raising our children alone. What if I fuck them up? What if I fail them? I feel like I failed you and all I want is to hold you one more time." I sobbed. My lips wet and salty from fallen tears.

"CJ, would you be willing to try something?" the leader asked. I nodded.

"I want you to imagine picking up Ariana and holding her in your arms. So, just reach over and pick her up."

Still with my eyes closed, I became consciously aware of the energy in the room again. It felt like we were all connected, experiencing this moment together on the most visceral level. We were all feeling this together.

I opened my eyes, looked across from me, leaned over and stretched my arms out to "pick her up." As I began to bring my arms back, I said aloud, while struggling to "lift her", "Damn Ariana, the afterlife isn't treating you so well. You're so heavy now." The energy in the room erupted as everyone began laughing. I smiled and for the first time, I experienced Ariana through laughter, through joy, in the ways we used to be.

I finished my second time in the circle and became cemented as "the guy who went twice." By the last day, the comfort and solace we all felt around each other was at its peak. We closed out the weekend with a burning ceremony. We were given instructions to write a letter to whomever we desired, something we need to forgive ourselves for, or something we had to release guilt about. I wrote to Ariana.

After finishing writing our letters, we all went outside and stood around a large stock pot. One by one, we read our letters aloud to the group. Then we would walk to the pot, light the letter on fire, and watch it burn. A symbolic and visceral way to release ourselves.

When it was my turn, I cried my way through the reading. Barely able to speak. My legs quivering, I walked to the stock pot, lit the letter on fire and began to sob. Feeling so vulnerable and so deeply affected by the weekend. The man, whose hands had first held me, walked over to me and held me in his arms one last time as I cried in his chest watching the letter burn.

The weekend ended, the same way it began. Crying in his arms.

We all packed up, said our goodbyes and coordinated

rides back to the airport. I left, altered, both emotionally and physically. I was transformed, and it broke me open to begin experiencing my grief in a new way. It showed me that I could walk through the fire and come out the other side. And so, I flew home, ran into the house and hugged my kids.

That weekend felt like years of therapy compressed into an intense, transformative experience. I learned what it meant to be truly seen, to be supported, to be vulnerable. I began to move my knowledge of grief into the experiential knowledge that grief is not something to be conquered, but a landscape to be navigated with compassion, with community, and with radical honesty.

When I returned, something had fundamentally shifted. I was learning to be present. The vision of the future began to show dim outlines, and for the first time since Ariana died I felt a small, nascent feeling that there could be life after grief. Not a life that erases the pain, but a life that integrates it and transforms it.

And while the retreat gave me a new way of experiencing my grief and offered a glimpse of hope, the journey was far from over. That weekend created the space I needed to finally confront the deeper, underlying battles that had long been intertwined with my sorrow.

THE DIAGNOSIS

I have lived with various degrees of depression and anxiety

throughout most of my life. The journey with my mental health is a long and arduous one. For so long, grief took a front seat and overshadowed and overtook my mental health. Because grief was so ever-present in my life and so strong, it was difficult to tease apart any other challenges in the realm of mental health.

It wasn't until life began to open up more and my capacity to hold my grief grew that I could begin to see the underlying battles of my mind through the cracks in the shell of my grief. The deeper my exploration, the more critical understanding my mental health became to understanding my grief. For sixteen years, I had been in therapy, working through trauma and character defects. In the four years after Ariana died, I tried almost every possible approach, ranging from standard therapies to more esoteric practices. Each profound, but something always felt incomplete.

As grief settled into my system, I emerged long enough to examine my mental health and the structure of my mind. I began to address each area of my life that grief had impacted and to understand how it amplified my existing mental patterns.

I would have these intense breakthroughs in therapy. Many times over, I would gain new understandings of the nature of my mind and body. It felt like progress, but there was a deep motivation in me to keep pushing, that something was still unexplained to me beneath the surface of everything I had been exploring.

At the beginning of 2024 I decided to take some time off from therapy and all therapeutic interventions. I was beginning to spiral at every tiny thought, and I felt I needed time to integrate all that I had learned over the past few years. It wasn't until the fall of 2024, when confronted with an intense sexual anxiety, linked with health anxiety, that I sought help again.

I began working with a new therapist and digging into so much more than just the anxiety. Specializing in trauma, she began to shine a light into my shadow in a way that I had not experienced before. After a few months, I walked into a session and said, "I think I'm depressed." She gently laughed and said, "Yeah, you're absolutely depressed." It was a moment of revelation. The way my depression presented was not the same as it had been in my past. It felt as though my grief was masking my depression and moments of "sadness" were hiding the anger I was feeling.

We continued our sessions, until one session, after a moment of pause, she said, "That's the anger, I just saw it. Right there. You need to let that out. I'm going to say something you won't want to hear, but you're ready. Even though she had no choice, to your nervous system, Ariana abandoned you. She left you. It's time to be angry about that and let it out."

I clenched my fists and shook my head 'no'. It was difficult to think any negative thoughts towards Ariana since her death. She had been elevated to sainthood in my mind. Her death washed away all her failures, and the residue of them seeped into me downstream. I was wrong. She was right. Always.

But I sat there for a minute. I closed my eyes and let the words linger and fall into me. My stomach constricted. My fist clenched tighter. I opened my eyes and said, "She abandoned me. She left me alone. With the kids. With no help. She left me. And I am angry at her for it. It's not fucking fair. She fucking left me," I cried.

For the rest of the session, I sat with that anger and all the guilt that was being poured over me. Before we finished the session, she had one more thing to tell me, "You have OCD as well as your depression. This is a recurring pattern that has come up over the course of our work together. It's clear and obvious. I know you mentioned medication before. It might be time to revisit the idea. While it is your choice, I will be in full support if you choose to go on meds. I believe it will be life changing for you." I was immediately nauseous. I pushed her words away and left the session as fast as I could.

Over the years, I had developed a crippling health anxiety that intensified after Ariana's death. It consumed me. Twenty-four hours a day. Hauntingly irrational thoughts would spiral and convince me I was dying, that I had cancer, that a terminal disease was lurking just beneath the surface. Every minor health concern became a catastrophic rumination.

The idea of taking medication was too overwhelming. After watching Ariana's medical journey and my son's tumor diagnosis, I had become afraid of even the simplest medications. I feared phone calls from doctors and driving past medical offices. The trauma had created a deep-seated fear of anything medical.

I sat with her words for a couple of weeks until my mental state became too overwhelming to handle on my own. So, I gave in and scheduled an appointment with a psychiatrist. At the end of my intake with the psychiatrist, I suddenly heard the same three letters repeated back to me: "O.C.D.". To confirm, we began doing a deeper evaluation and testing. A few weeks later, I was on a call with my psychiatrist when it was confirmed: I had OCD.

As the screen faded, my mind immediately began examining every memory I could recall through the lens of this diagnosis, reliving painful experiences and watching myself from the outside. I observed, and suddenly—and this is not hyperbole—my entire self made sense.

This diagnosis was more than just a label for me. It was an explanation for my entire life experience. I began studying OCD and learned about my subtype "Pure O" and "Relationship OCD." I discovered that my compulsions often existed only in my mind, that the symptoms were far more encompassing and insidious than I had ever realized.

After a time of grieving, I encountered the most challenging part–I had to accept that I couldn't control my OCD through willpower alone. For sixteen years, I had believed I could push through therapy, utilize supplements, and rely on willpower to "heal myself." I believed I could be in total control, but medication meant giving up control, and that terrified me. I didn't know what taking medication would do to my body and my brain.

Yet, I knew the only path forward for me was to go on medicine to begin finding a more peaceful existence. I went on the first medication, and after six months it enabled me to breathe for what felt like the first time in my life. I could focus. I could feel deep pain, and I was no longer caught in rumination and fear for hours or sometimes days on end. The compulsions began to slow down and weaken. I found myself able to observe them and see them in an entirely new way.

THE GIFT

For most of the last four years, swimming in my grief was my default state. I used to believe that staying in suffering kept me connected to Ariana. Logically, I knew I could remain connected through joy and love, but emotionally, it felt impossible; my work with my company Unvoiced and other projects meant I was constantly surrounded by grief, which became both a comfort and a trap.

Healthy grieving, I learned, is about sitting in the discomfort. It's about being curious about your pain, allowing your body to process emotions without numbing or distracting. I started practicing this by giving shape and color to my grief; imagining it as something tangible, whether a basketball-sized sensation in my chest or a spiky entity in my stomach.

The longer I sat in the discomfort, the more vivid the difference between pain and suffering became. Suffering would show up as resistance to, judgment of, and an attempt to rid myself of the pain I was experiencing. It is all the stories I would tell myself about my loss, about my trauma and pain. It is my belief in what I can and cannot handle. Grief is painful enough; it became important to be with my pain and to resist suffering.

Slowly, gratitude began to enter the experience. Early on, the concept of gratitude journals and toxic positivity made me furious. How could I be grateful when I was shattered? But over time, I learned that gratitude isn't about manufacturing positivity. It's about acknowledging even tiny moments of presence and connection.

Over time, my relationship with Ariana transformed and

moments of presence and gratitude increased. Instead of trying to maintain a physical connection, I learned to love her on a different plane. I knew we had a love that transcended physical reality. It existed in a sacred spot in my heart, reserved just for her, with expanded capacity and room for new experiences, new love, and a new future.

One of the most significant insights is that the gift of grief is personal and cannot be rushed. It emerges as you grow your capacity to hold contradictory emotions; joy and sorrow existing simultaneously. For me, the gift was both tangible and intangible.

Tangibly, it meant founding new businesses, creating platforms like Unvoiced, Hopeless Mope, and The Day After. These weren't just professional ventures, but expressions of my transformed understanding of pain, community, and healing. They allowed me avenues to express my grief, suffering, and pain outwardly through artistic endeavors and creating a mission that no griever would be alone in their journey. I realized how insufficient our world was at talking about, expressing, and handling grief. No one knew how to talk to me, and I didn't know how to talk to them. I decided after some time to go all in, leaving my twenty-year career in Tech behind, and dedicated my life to bringing grief out of the shadows. Unvoiced gave me the chance to create a community that supports and encourages growth. It allowed me the opportunity to affect the way our corporate culture handles grief in their organizations. With story at the core of it all.

I believe, wholly, that story is the most powerful thing we have as humans. It builds empathy and understanding. It is why I wrote this book, and it is why I keep stories at the heart of everything we do at Unvoiced. Sharing my story during my time at Facebook was the catalyst for a company-wide policy being created for those needing time off for medical reasons. It was the first time I saw the power of stories. Hearing others, creating art and clothing, and building platforms to share others' stories has become one of the single greatest outlets for processing my grief and the most rewarding way to spend my time. I wake up each day, so incredibly grateful to get to do what I do.

Intangibly, the gift was far more profound. I came to a deep self-love, something I had spent the better part of my life struggling to find.

I spent years in complete self-hatred. My motivation was driven by a desperate need to prove I wasn't "a piece of shit." Success was a way to combat my internal narrative of unworthiness. But something shifted; my motivation transformed from proving my worth to being motivated for the purpose of experiencing pleasure, joy, and service to others.

Looking in the mirror became an act of radical acceptance. I could finally say, without irony or self-contempt, that I am worthy of love and joy. This might sound simple, but for someone who had lived with deep-seated self-hatred, it was revolutionary.

Community became my lifeline. I became intentional about finding people who could provide support and love, but who would also challenge me. I needed people who could hold space for my darkest moments, who wouldn't let me hide from my pain. People I could be fully honest with, who could hear anything, even from the darkest recesses of my shadow.

The specific lessons of my journey are not prescriptive.

They are merely a testament to the individual nature of grief. Find your community. Learn to recognize when you're swimming in grief, versus experiencing it. Confront your grief with curiosity. Hold strong boundaries and remember that you don't owe anyone an explanation for your feelings.

You are allowed to find joy and peace while still carrying your grief. You can be happy and sad. You can be joyful and sorrowful. You can move forward, bringing your grief along as a changed partner in your life.

The container we hold for our grief grows proportionately to the joy and love we can experience. As I worked to expand my capacity to hold grief, I found myself capable of experiencing joy, pleasure, and love in ways I never thought possible.

To those overwhelmed by grief: start exactly where you are. Acknowledge the overwhelm. Get curious about it. Begin with five seconds of presence, then ten. Build your capacity slowly. Your body has its own wisdom, and reconnecting takes time.

I'm hesitant to predict the future. The past four years have been nothing like I could have imagined. Who would have thought I'd be running these businesses, leaving my career in tech behind, publishing a book, and creating entirely new paths? Each step has been about being as honest as I could be with myself and those around me.

The best possible future we can imagine pales in comparison to what might actually unfold. If my younger self could have seen the life I'm living now, he would never have believed it. Even in his wildest longings and desires, this future I walk forward with optimism. Not a toxic, forced positivity, but a genuine openness to possibility. My relationship with grief continues to evolve. I continue to make mistakes and I continue to fail myself, my children, and the beautiful people in my life.

But this is not an ending. It is a continuation. A journey of growing love, of expanding capacity, of carrying forward both pain and joy. A renewed sense of forgiveness and self-love each day I am allowed to exist.

To anyone reading this: your grief is sacred. It is yours alone. There is no roadmap, no perfect way to navigate this landscape of loss. Some days, you will feel like you're drowning. Other days, you'll feel a strange, unexpected lightness. Both are valid. Both are part of your journey.

Grief is not something to be conquered, but a companion to understand. It is not your life, but a part of your life. And in learning to hold it, to grow with it, you might just discover something profound about yourself.

This is not an ending.
This is a beginning.

- CJ Infantino
Widower. Father. Son.
A New Person.

The man who carried me in his arms all weekend and stirred my heart and supported me. He allowed me to express my rage and pain. I will always be indebted to him, and he will always have my love, along with the other men who willingly shared my pain.

CJ INFANTINO

TORN PAGES FROM A BROKEN HEART

CJ Infantino lives in Upstate New York with his three children. After enduring the painful isolation of losing his wife and feeling lost in his grief, he decided to take action and work to bring grief out of the shadows. This inspired him to leave nearly two decades of work as an engineer in the tech industry to found *Unvoiced, a mission-driven company* dedicated to transforming how we discuss grief, supporting those who are grieving, and fostering more compassionate spaces in both work and life.

About the Author

CJ Infantino is the founder of Unvoiced, a mission-driven company dedicated to changing how we talk about grief and building more compassionate spaces. He lives in New York with his three children.

Connect With Us

CJ Infantino
Meta & LinkedIn: @CJINFANTINO
Email: HELLO@UNVOICED.COM

Unvoiced
YouTube & Meta: @UNVOICEDCO
TikTok: @UNVOICED_GRIEFTALKS

Resources & Related Work

Unvoiced
Dedicated to changing the world of grief and supporting those who grieve. Learn more or get in touch:
UNVOICED.COM

Unvoiced Merch & Hopeless Mope
Wear your feelings. Matter. Support the cause through our clothing:
SHOP.UNVOICED.COM